More Than A Lemonade Stand™

More Than A Lemonade Stand™

*The Complete Guide for Planning,
Implementing & Running a Successful
Youth Entrepreneur Camp*

Julie Ann Wood

New York

More Than A Lemonade Stand™
The Complete Guide for Planning, Implementing & Running a Successful Youth Entrepreneur Camp

Published in New York, New York, by Morgan James Publishing. Morgan James and The Entrepreneurial Publisher are trademarks of Morgan James, LLC. www.MorganJamesPublishing.com

The Morgan James Speakers Group can bring authors to your live event. For more information or to book an event visit The Morgan James Speakers Group at www.TheMorganJamesSpeakersGroup.com.

A free eBook edition is available
with the purchase of this print book.

CLEARLY PRINT YOUR NAME ABOVE IN UPPER CASE

Instructions to claim your free eBook edition:
1. Download the BitLit app for Android or iOS
2. Write your name in **UPPER CASE** on the line
3. Use the BitLit app to submit a photo
4. Download your eBook to any device

ISBN 9781630474546 paperback
ISBN 9781630474553 eBook
ISBN 9781630474560 hardcover
Library of Congress Control Number:
2014917774

Cover Design by:
Rachel Lopez
www.r2cdesign.com

Interior Design by:
Bonnie Bushman
bonnie@caboodlegraphics.com

Original Lemonade Stand graphic
created by Kyle Wood

In an effort to support local communities, raise awareness and funds, Morgan James Publishing donates a percentage of all book sales for the life of each book to Habitat for Humanity Peninsula and Greater Williamsburg.

Get involved today, visit
www.MorganJamesBuilds.com

Habitat
for Humanity
Peninsula and
Greater Williamsburg
Building Partner

Table of Contents

||||||||||||||||||||||||||||||||||||||||||||||

Dear Reader
||||||||||||||||||||||||||||||||

Think back to when you were a child. Remember the time when you decided to raise a little extra spending money by opening up your own lemonade stand? Maybe your mom or dad helped raise funds for you by loaning you the grocery store money to buy the lemons, sugar, and cups. Or maybe you just syphoned off the cartons of lemonade your parents brought home from the store. Regardless of how you made it happen, this was probably the beginning of your entrepreneurial career. A lemonade stand could be anything. It could be selling baseball cards, video games, mowing the neighbor's lawn, babysitting, or, as you grow, beginning a new business or company. But the important thing to note is that a lemonade stand is grounded in the desire to build youth entrepreneurship at a young age to better prepare our children for exciting opportunities in life. The sooner we educate and train the new generation in fundamental business practices, the better positioned they will be to succeed in the hyper-competitive business world.

Just as technology is used as a tool to accomplish more in less time, youth entrepreneurship can be used as the tool to develop youth in less time. This book focuses on a proven youth entrepreneurship curriculum to help kids utilize their unique talents and skills to start a business, creating by-products of increased confidence and self-esteem. Through the experiential learning activities included in the curriculum, they will learn basic business terms, learn how a business runs, develop their own business idea and participate in a large team lemonade stand competition to raise money for a scholarship fund. These activities are so fun and engaging that kids don't even realize that they are learning until they attend the awards ceremony and see the results they've achieved.

More Than a Lemonade Stand™ is a complete step-by-step guide to planning, implementing and running a successful youth entrepreneur camp. This book provides a thorough explanation of the activities that I complete each year for the youth entrepreneur camp that I direct at the University of Wisconsin – Madison Small Business Development Center. This guide is for anyone from seasoned trainers/teachers to parents, science centers, museums, youth centers, small business development centers, community education programs, or other organizations that would like to implement a youth entrepreneur camp or incorporate youth entrepreneur curriculum into their current programs.

The book is set up as a checklist so that you can use it as a resource year after year as you start planning and implementing an activity or program. It can also be used to train your staff and as a communication tool so that everyone understands the what, why, and how to. Even though More Than a Lemonade Stand™ is set up in a camp format, the book is designed so that you can pull the activities out and use them in any program that focuses on youth entrepreneurship. The activities are geared for kids in grades 5-8, but with minor modification I have used them for as young as 3rd and 4th grade and as high as 11th grade.

The activities are synergistic in that they build and reinforce each other to help increase the kids' entrepreneurial skills, confidence, and self-image. This is done by focusing on developing the kids' unique passions and interests, with the goal of turning them into viable business ideas that they are equipped to run when they leave the camp. The Biz Ops Game™ and the Lemonade Stand Team competition not only add to the fun and engagement of the activities, but they also increase their entrepreneurial skills and self-image as they utilize their strengths to contribute to the team and make it a successful business.

I have yet to find a complete book that includes both the planning and implementing of a youth entrepreneur curriculum, which also gives the reader the option to plug in and use with existing programs, or as one complete curriculum. There are hundreds, if not thousands, of business startup books written specifically for adults who are starting or running a business that are viable options for teachers to research and use to create their own youth entrepreneur curriculum. There are also several business startup books that are written for kids and there are even a few books that are written for parents that are designed to teach business to their kids. There are a few curriculums available for teachers to use in their classrooms, but those are mostly semester long classes that are geared toward high school aged kids or younger kids. The middle school aged kids are for some reason missed; these are transition years for kids and since they are too young to get a job as an employee, it is a great age to start a business. More Than A Lemonade Stand™ is the only book that offers a complete curriculum designed for all age groups.

Another way that More Than A Lemonade Stand™ is different is that it is a completely experiential learning curriculum. Just as entrepreneurship is all about experiential learning, so are the hands-on learning activities in this book. This book is not just about entrepreneurship—it is also about utilizing entrepreneurship as a tool to develop youth into more confident, more creative, and more responsible individuals that make the world a better place. If you make a commitment to utilize the curriculum presented in this book, I promise you will begin to make a positive difference in the development of youth in your area.

This entrepreneurship program will help kids make the connection between math, reading, teamwork, communication, and the real life experience of running a business. The entrepreneurial mindset taught in this program helps kids realize and utilize their gifts and talents to solve today's problems so that they can help make our lives better.

Teaching entrepreneurship as a viable career option will help the US economy. The US Bureau of Labor Statistics stated that unemployment for youth ages 16-24 rose to 19.7 million in July of 2013; only 50.7% of that age group was employed in July 2013 at the peak of summer employment. Teaching kids about entrepreneurship empowers them to create their own job when they are unable to find one. The Small Business Administration (SBA) reports that small businesses make up over half of the private workforce in the US, yet many of the skills needed to create successful entrepreneurs are not taught in schools. Exposing kids to entrepreneurship at a young age increases the chances that they see this as a possible profession.

Implementing the Lemonade Stand activities will show kids how they can give back and make a difference. I believe strongly in giving back and that is why the team Lemonade Stand competition is set up to raise funds for youth entrepreneur camp scholarships. The friendly Lemonade Stand competition helps the kids understand that not everyone can afford an activity and there are ways that they can take action and help. Also, 10% of sales of any More Than a Lemonade Stand™ product from my website will go to support a cure for childhood cancer (in honor of my brother Jeff whose entrepreneurial flame was extinguished far too early).

I look forward to the weeklong camp that I run each summer, as it is the most fulfilling and rewarding experience I have each year. It is amazing to see kids come in Monday morning who are quiet, lack self-confidence, and who are not excelling in the traditional school classroom transform through the week and leave on Friday afternoon feeling confident and ready to go run their business. The benefits the students receive from the camp are so incredible that I feel compelled to share the blueprints of how to build your own successful youth camp. This book is for anyone who wants to try using entrepreneurship as a tool, and I guarantee that implementing the More Than a Lemonade Stand™ curriculum will provide a rewarding experience!

Acknowledgements

||||||||||||||||||||||||||||||||||||||||||||||||||||||

There are definitely a lot of people that help make a book a success, especially when it involves decades of experiences and learning to build the knowledge that created it. So with that said, I want to thank all my teachers, co-workers, bosses, employees and friends who have helped me grow and learn over the years, and also all the youth entrepreneurship camp staff and campers that I have worked with who have helped me grow and who give me such a joy-filled week!

I would like to thank my parents for raising me in an entrepreneurial environment and showing me that I could create and do whatever I put my mind to. To my brothers, who were my students when we played school and who put up with my bossiness. To my children, who are the greatest gift of my life and who provide me with more happiness than I could have ever imagined. And lastly, to my husband, who not only accepts my dreams, but also helps make them come true.

What's to Come
||||||||||||||||||||||||||||||||||||||||||||

Before we dive headfirst into the world of youth entrepreneurship, I felt it important to offer you as the reader a roadmap for what is to come. More Than a Lemonade Stand™ offers readers the opportunity to build a leadership-based and business-oriented program for our young entrepreneurs. To help achieve this goal, this book is broken down into three specific and detailed sections. They all play a crucial role in the journey, but each has their own independent message and purpose.

The three sections include:

Section I: Countdown to Camp

The first section of the book is all about the front end planning that needs to be done before camp begins. Just like any large event that takes place; planning is the #1 most important thing you can do to hold a successful camp. Proper planning prevents you from fighting fires and reacting to situations that may come up just before, or even worse during, the camp. Just like the Boy Scout motto states, it is always good to "be prepared!"

The planning section contains all aspects of the planning process, which include the logistics, fundraising, staffing, budgeting, pricing and marketing of the camp. It also includes what supplies are needed for the camp and what forms are necessary. Many of the forms and documents are included in this book to use as a guide that you can adapt to your unique situation.

The planning section is organized by time so that you can see what needs to be done when, ensuring you don't miss any important details. The planning section can be used as a base for planning not only for the More Than a Lemonade Stand™ program, but also for any event or program that requires an event planning process.

Section II: Camp Curriculum: And Now the Fun Begins

The second section of the book focuses on what takes place during the camp. The curriculum section includes a detailed explanation of the activities used and how to implement them into the camp or in your own unique program. It breaks down the days into chunks by type of activity so that this section can be used as the proposed camp schedule, or as a plug and play into an existing program. It includes time frames and learning objectives so you know the purpose of each activity in order to make it easy to fit into your unique situation. There is a sample pre- and post-test that can be used to measure not only students' progress, but also their self-perceptions. This section will provide specific step-by-step procedures for running the business simulation and lemonade stand competition activities. It will also include the 'how to' for creating the materials necessary to implement the activities into your program.

The section will include where to find guest speakers and field trip locations, and which types of speakers and businesses make the best ones for middle-school aged kids. This section also takes you through the curriculum used to develop the campers' business ideas and the format that I have found to work best. Relevant games and other short activities are explained so that they can be used to fill in shorter time periods and enhance the curriculum. The proven success formula for teaching business subjects to the middle age group is revealed, and details of why it works are explained. Also included is how to run an awards poster ceremony for friends and family of the campers, and why it is a great ending to the week's activities.

Section III: Executing the Plan: Building Memories

By this point, you have worked enormously hard to implement and execute your curriculum. Executing the plan takes this one step further and focuses on The Biz Ops Game™, which is a fun and engaging business simulation that teaches campers the basics of the day-to-day operations of running a manufacturing and retail business. Outside of having a great experience and making new friends, the goal of any Lemonade Stand Camp should be to execute The Biz Ops Game™ in a manner that supports a real-life business model and builds amazing memories to inspire your campers to grow into entrepreneurs.

Much like a real business, this piece of the curriculum (along with the lemonade stand) will help campers get a feel for what is expected when running a business. They will have to make difficult business decisions, budget, market, and promote their company. But most importantly, it will help to build memories and a rush of excitement for campers. Win, lose, or draw, these campers participating in the competition will be better prepared to make sound and informed business decisions later in life.

Section IV: Breathe: After the Camp is Over

The third section discusses the importance of camp evaluations both from the camper and the parent perspective. It includes determining the best time to capture the information, as well as sample questions to use in the evaluations. The section includes instructions on how to run a debrief session with the current staff so improvements can be made for the next camp. It also includes hints and tips for storing items for next year's camp, complete with inventory worksheets.

The goal of this section is to take the time to evaluate your camp to not only learn from your successes, but also your missteps. Obtaining camper feedback and data is crucial to being able to determine where you can improve. Just like in any business setting, you should constantly be measuring your progress to ensure that your lemonade stand is always the brightest and most welcoming one.

Throughout this book, you will see the image of a burning flame, entitled *Campfire Wisdom*. Each of these campfires carries quick and helpful tidbits learned through years of experience from hosting these camps and building youth entrepreneurial programs. They should not only help prevent you from getting burned, but also shed light on some of the most valuable pieces of advice this book offers.

Campfire Wisdom: Hints and tips learned through experience that will help you avoid learning the hard way.

Finally, the last piece to this book is the included free membership site and online resources. Here, you can download forms and checklists referenced in the book. The site will provide more in-depth resources and information to help you create your own entrepreneurial youth camp. There is also a message board where users can upload their own helpful guidance, advice, experience, and stories from their own lives. It truly takes a village, and this site will offer you additional tools to help you create a meaningful experience for your campers.

You can go to: http://eseedling.com/more-than-a-lemonade-stand-book/book-resources and use the password: **MoreLemonade** to download and use the forms for your program.

Section I

Countdown to Camp
||||||||||||||||||||||||||||||||||||||||||||||||||||||||

A s mentioned above, Section 1 focuses on the steps you'll need to take to prepare for your campers. Much of the success and missteps that occur during your time with campers can be traced back to your planning. If you take the time and effort on the details needed to build a successful camp, you'll quickly find traction in the form of engaged and excited campers. It takes time and organization to develop a meaningful opportunity for these young entrepreneurs, but is well worth it when you see how completely dedicated and eager they are to get started.

Planning – The Earlier the Better!

Planning is the #1 most important thing you can do to create a successful camp experience for everyone involved including staff, parents, campers and presenters. For example, the earlier you start, the more supplies you can gather for free or buy at lower prices, the more donors you can contact, the more awareness you can create, and the more campers you will have in attendance. This section takes the guesswork out of putting together the camp. As an added bonus, you will find a planning and implementation checklist organized by time frame, so that you know what needs to be done when. The entire planning section is organized in the same manner by mirroring the checklist. If you follow the time frames and order of tasks as recommended in this section it will save you the time and energy you would spend figuring out what to do next, and it will allow you to achieve your goal of putting on a successful camp much faster. The checklist is like a map so that you can see how far you have progressed and how much further you have to go. It will also help you to see any potential problems that might arise along the way, and it will help you to quickly remedy them. It is much easier to make adjustments to your plan than to deal with a crisis during the camp.

 Campfire Wisdom: Download a free planning & implementation checklist at http://eseedling. com/more-than-a-lemonade-stand-book/book-resources and use the password: **MoreLemonade**

The best way to consider your planning of the curriculum is from a time perspective and checklist perspective. Take a look at the following checklist for your More Than a Lemonade Stand™ camp:

More Than a Lemonade Stand™ Camp
Planning & Implementation Checklist

There are many steps to take before your camp actually begins. The devil is truly in the details, and you'll find the more prepared you are to handle the small issues, the more successful you'll find your camper's experience. Thus, consider the following tasks and timeframes as you prepare for day one.

What Should You Do Before Camp Begins

Six Months Before

❒ **Name your camp and create a logo!**
In order to successfully market your camp, you will need a name and design for all marketing materials including t-shirts. You might be asking yourself, do I really need a logo? The answer is 100% yes, and in order to further convince you, here are five reasons why a logo is necessary:

1) People judge a book by its cover – so create a good first impression.
2) It gives extra credibility that promotes your camp as being big and established.
3) It shows that you are reputable – parents really like to know their kids are going to a camp they can trust.

4) It builds your individual identity – the logo is just the beginning of your brand and all your materials should complement each other.

5) It shows commitment to what you are doing.

A logo should convey the vision you have for the camp. If you are an existing organization that is creating a camp you will need to take into consideration your company's professional appearance. You will also want to think about colors, font choices, style, size, and placement when creating a logo. These all have a part in communicating your brand to your audience.

It is always good to have feedback from prospective customers and co-workers on your design and name. This will help you validate that your design conveys what you are trying to communicate, and ultimately it will make your design better. How early you start will determine how much feedback you have time to gather. At minimum, you should work on the logo one year to six months before the camp is scheduled so that you can create marketing materials (more on that in the marketing section) and effectively promote the camp.

You may also want to create a website (or page if you are adding the camp to part of an existing organization). You don't have to be extremely creative; you just need to communicate what you are selling to your customers. The camp name can be as simple as *your organization name's* Youth Entrepreneur Camp.

Campfire Wisdom: You have the option of purchasing the More than a Lemonade Stand™ t-shirts and gear; go to www.MoreThanALemonadeStand.com for more information.

❑ Reserve a venue

You may already have space to hold the camp at your organization, but if you don't then you need to reserve a room to be used as the base and main classroom for your camp. Popular venues fill up many months (if not years) in advance so it is important to find a place early in the planning process. Prices and amenities can vary significantly, so it is advised to check on at least three different venues that provide the following items needed for the camp:

1) Room set up for number of campers (24-25 is the ideal size) with 6 tables of 4 each with chairs that can be moved around for different activities. If you want a larger camp, you could have 5 chairs at each table. I would recommend 25 as the maximum number of kids allowed in the camp. I've dealt with up to 32 and have found 25 to be much more manageable. If you do want to allow for a larger group, you will need to think about having 3 teams for the Lemonade Stand Competition and adding more staff.

2) Parking for parents to drop off, pick up, and attend the poster session on the last day. Parking is also nice to have for the presenters and staff.

3) A place that the kids can hold their Lemonade Stand Competition (and where there are actually customers to sell to).

4) A computer lab (this is for the campers to work on their business presentations and business cards), unless you require them to bring a laptop or have enough laptops for each camper to use.

5) Catering, if you are planning on providing lunch and snacks for the campers, or if they don't have catering, whether or not they allow food to be brought in (external catering).

 Campfire Wisdom: Many venues have a lower rate for nonprofit organizations. If you are a nonprofit, check with the venue as it could save you quite a bit of money.

❏ Pricing the camp

When pricing your camp, you first need to identify the objective of your camp. Is it to give back to the community, is it to support another part of your program, is it to make a profit, or is it just to cover your costs? You will also want to check the prices of the other summer camps in your area that target the same age group and offer the same amenities (i.e. day camp with lunch). Parents on a budget will look at several camp options and may opt for a lower price camp if your fees are higher. To price your camp you have to take into consideration all of the costs, which is why you want to start planning early. You will want to create a budget for the camp; below is a sample budget that you can use as a guide. You will also need to consider whether or not you would like to offer scholarships for low-income families and if so, decide if your budget will cover these scholarships or if you will find sponsors.

SAMPLE BUDGET SPREADSHEET FOR THE CAMP
More Than a Lemonade Stand™
Youth Entrepreneur Camp
Sample Budget Spreadsheet

Description
Marketing Pieces
Mailing Costs
Advertising/Promotion
Canvas Brief Case - (Could substitute drawstring backpack if want lower cost)
T-Shirt
Water Bottle
Business Cards -Avery computer forms (2 sheets per camper)
Certificate Paper (1 per camper)
Poster Tri-fold boards for poster presentations
Poster paper for lemonade stand, other lemonade stand supplies
Binder for workbook materials
Paper for workbook materials
Cost for Copies
Magic Markers, Paper, Scissors, Crayons, Pens
Pad folios with calculators (could use notebooks for less cost)
Supplies to Create Simulation (included in the curriculum section)

Instructor Pay (recommend min. of 1 per 10 students; ideally 2 per 10 students)

Venue Cost (or room rental fee)

Computer Lab Rental

Food Costs

Marketing/Promotional Costs

Total Budget

 Campfire Wisdom: The Team Lemonade Stand competition usually makes approximately $100 in net profits that can be used to pay for camp supplies or camp scholarships.

❒ **Finding sponsors for your camp**

If you need help funding your camp, you will want to find sponsors. Fortunately, youth entrepreneurship is an area where many entrepreneurs want to help. You will need to set a goal of how much money you would like to raise. From experience, I have found that sponsors want choices for how much they should give, so I would recommend creating a menu of options for levels of sponsorship. They also want to know what you will give them for their money, so be sure to include that in your menu of options. Below is a sample that you can use as a guideline when developing your own sponsorship levels. Some additional options might be t-shirt sponsors and awards ceremony sponsors. Writing a grant is another option you have for raising funds for your camp. You can search for youth entrepreneurship grants and see if there are any current ones that fit your criteria. But, I have found finding sponsors to be much easier to acquire over writing a grant and waiting to see if you are funded. This is the main reason why I focus on sponsors for fundraising.

To find sponsors in your area, it is always better to have a personal contact that can tell you exactly what to do to apply for the funds. If you don't have a personal contact, go to corporations who have home offices in your area and search for their foundation or community page; they usually list what type of groups they support and how to submit your information.

More Than a Lemonade Stand™
Youth Entrepreneur Camp Sponsorship Opportunities

Camp Sponsor $2,500.00 (1 available)
- Guest speaker to students on business topic OR Field trip stop at your location
- Attendance at student lunch or break
- Logo on t-shirt and briefcase
- Name on sponsorship list given to students/parents
- Name and logo on website sponsorship list
- Attendance and recognition at closing reception

Lemonade Stand Team Sponsor $1,500.00 (2 available)
- Option to serve as a mentor to student lemonade stand project
- Logo announcing sponsorship at lemonade stand
- Logo on t-shirt
- Name on sponsorship list given to students/parents

- Name and logo on website sponsorship list
- Attendance and recognition at closing reception

Lunch Sponsor $500.00 (5 available)
- Provide a company overview at lunch to students
- Logo or banner provided by company placed at lunch
- Name on sponsorship list given to students/parents
- Name on website sponsorship list
- Attendance and recognition at closing reception

Student Sponsor $325.00 (10 available)
- Business name on student name-tag
- Name on sponsorship list given to students/parents
- Name on website sponsorship list
- Attendance and recognition at closing reception

Friend of Youth Entrepreneur Camp Sponsor suggested donation $100.00
- Name on sponsorship list given to students/parents
- Name on website sponsorship list
- Attendance and recognition at closing reception

Make sure you implement some sort of follow-up program as well, focusing on the feedback provided to ensure you can generate scholarships, or at least know why your contacts chose not to support your cause. This can be done through direct calls or emails or even the inclusion of a prepaid postcard with specific boxes your potential donor can check.

❐ Staffing the camp

Staffing your camp with confident, patient adults who have positive outlooks is the 2nd most important thing for running a successful camp (remember, planning was #1). The camp staff is what makes or breaks the campers experience, and creating a great camp experience is what is going to get you testimonials and word of mouth recommendations—two extremely important things if you want your camp to fill year after year.

If you are using your organization's existing staff for the camp, it is best to utilize their strengths. If you have staff that already works with kids in an existing program, they are the first ones to utilize. It is amazing to me how many adults are hesitant to help out because the camp is for kids. It is important for the staff to feel comfortable working with kids or they will have trouble communicating and encouraging them. Utilizing your current staff's strengths will help them feel more successful and confident in working with middle-school aged kids.

If you have someone who is a project manager, then they might be a great person to do the planning. If you have someone with financial expertise, they could teach the financial unit in the camp and help students with lemonade stand finances. If you have a marketing person, they can help market the camp and then teach the marketing content to the campers.

If you are hiring staff, take into account their experience working with middle-school aged kids and their business background. A group to target when looking for potential staff, if you have to hire them, is college students that might be majoring in entrepreneurship or business, or who may have counseled at a scout or leadership camp. Other people who make good camp staff are current small business owners/ entrepreneurs and teachers who have the summer off. I have found that some even want to give back and volunteer for the camp.

For staffing ratios, I would recommend that you have at least 1 adult camp counselor for every 10 campers; ideally having 1 adult per 5 campers' works best. They don't all have to be in the camp at all times (minimum of 2 needed at all times), but the camp business curriculum is designed to teach 4 stations at one time. The reason you need to have at least 2 camp staff with the kids at all times is to reduce your liability against a "he said, she said" incident.

Always make sure you get a background check on camp staff (even if they are volunteers). Again this is to reduce your liability from anything that may come up that you could have prevented with a simple background check. You will also want to make sure that at least one person is certified in CPR and First Aid just in case something health related happens during the camp. You will also want to check any other legal staff requirements with your organization to make sure everything is covered.

❐ Create a brochure or promotional piece

Once you have sorted out all of the details of location and price, you can then create a marketing piece that communicates the details for the camp. When deciding if creating a brochure or promotional piece is necessary, you need to decide what it will be used for and when you will use it. Is mailing your prospects a leaflet the best way to communicate what you are offering, or is there a better way such as an email with the same content or an email directing them to your website? My thought is that it is always best to have a promotional piece created, especially if you are dealing with schools as a method of distributing your camp information. The school staff will then have something to give to students, and parents, who may be interested in attending.

If you have the expertise in your organization, you can create the brochure using a word processing program or a publishing program. If you have your sponsors before creating the promotional piece, you can put their logos and thank them for their support.

In the marketing piece you want to be sure to include:

- The location
- The dates
- Who can attend (i.e. what grade levels)
- The benefits
- A summary of the activities
- How to register (or include a registration form)
- The price
- Scholarship information
- Contact information
- Testimonials & photos (after the first year)

For an example of a one page promotional piece that you can use as a guide for your camp visit: http://eseedling.com/more-than-a-lemonade-stand-book/book-resources and use the password: **MoreLemonade**

❐ Create a Website or Update an Existing One With Camp Information

Your website is another way to communicate to your audience about your camp. It may also be the way in which people can register for it as well. Having specific information on your website will show your prospects (and sponsors) that you are serious and committed to making the camp a success.

If you have an existing website, you will want to make sure you update it with the camp information (similar to the promotional piece you created). If not, you will want to create one so that you can market your camp effectively online. Your budget and technology options will be the determining factors in how complicated your website will be. If you have someone on staff that can develop or update websites it will help keep the cost down.

Make sure you have a "call to action," which can be used to register for your camp, or make sure to include all of the details of how to register if they can't register on the website.

❐ Decide if you are offering scholarships

Camps are a great way to break down economic, racial, religious, ethnic and social barriers between kids, so I would recommend offering scholarships for low income students who could not otherwise afford to attend the camp. I believe that the kids learn even more when there is a diverse group. They learn to be more accepting of differences and come to realize that each camper can bring unique gifts and talents to the team.

To make sure that the kids applying are serious about wanting to participate and learn at camp, include a short application on why they want to attend the camp that they must complete to be considered. Eligibility for free or reduced hot lunch criteria is used for the scholarships; it seems to be the easiest and most non-invasive method there is in qualifying the applicants. You will need to decide how much of your budget you want to use for scholarships so you know how many scholarships you can offer. Below are sample scholarship guidelines, forms, and an application.

 Campfire Wisdom: Check with your local or state school organizations to see if there are scholarship programs based on income already in place. Your camp may qualify for some of the funds.

SAMPLE LETTER TO SEND TO SCHOOLS AND YOUTH ORGANIZATIONS
More Than a Lemonade Stand™
Youth Entrepreneur Camp and Scholarship Information

I would like to inform you of our 2014 dates for the More Than A Lemonade Stand™ Youth Entrepreneur Camp for students currently in 6ᵗʰ, 7ᵗʰ or 8ᵗʰ grades. The dates and times for this commuter day camp are _____ and it will be held at _____. Please share the camp information with students and teachers at your school (*NOTE: if sending to a youth organization change to students or parents*). Enclosed are five brochures and scholarship information *(if applicable)*, if you need more copies of either, please contact me at the information below.

(If you do have scholarship information – include the information in the letter so they know what is needed to qualify – such as free or reduced hot lunch).

The application forms for both scholarship programs are enclosed along with several camp brochures. Both scholarships are limited, so please encourage students to apply as soon as possible if they are interested in attending. Feel free to give me a call or email me if you have any questions.

Sincerely,

Julie Wood

Youth Entrepreneur Camp Director

More Than a Lemonade Stand™

Phone: 608-332-9836

Email: juliewood@eseedling.com

SAMPLE SCHOLARSHIP APPLICATION
More Than a Lemonade Stand™
Scholarship Program Application
YOUTH ENTREPRENEUR CAMP July 14-25, 2014

This is a needs based scholarship from E-seedling, LLC. To be eligible you must qualify for reduced or free hot lunch at your school. A parent or guardian must complete the information below and sign that the student qualifies for free or reduced hot lunch. Also, please review page 2 with your student, and have the student complete the brief statement on why they want to attend the camp and sign. This scholarship covers all but $50 of the fee, which is due by the start of the camp. The scholarships pay $275 and are limited, so please apply by May 1st for review. If you have any questions, please contact:

_____ at _____.

Return to:

_____

_____

_____

_____

I. Applicant Information

Name _____

Address _____

City _____ Zip code _____

Daytime telephone _____ Evening telephone _____

Email _____

How did you hear about the Youth Entrepreneur Camp Program?

II. Applicant Certification

I verify (by signing below) that my student qualifies for free or reduced meals at their school.

Name of school: _____

Parent/guardian signature _____

Date_____

Under federal scholarship tax laws, this scholarship may be considered taxable income.

More Than a Lemonade Stand™
Scholarship Program Application
YOUTH ENTREPRENEUR CAMP July 14-25, 2014

I, _____, want to participate in the More Than a Lemonade Stand Youth Entrepreneur Camp and receive a scholarship to attend. I am currently in 6th, 7th or 8th grade. By signing below, I agree to:

- Attend all days of the program
- Be on time and stay the full day
- Participate constructively in all required program activities
- Behave in a way that is respectful of others and the facility
- Follow all instructions from the instructor and staff

Please write a brief statement (50-100 words) about why you want to attend the Youth Entrepreneur Camp and receive a scholarship. This statement is required:

Student Signature _____

Date_____

❒ **Decide who to market to and gather contact information**

Once the brochure or promotional piece is completed, you need to determine whom you are going to target (and how much you want to spend on promotion). If you are an organization, you will probably want to start with your membership as this will be the most cost effective and easiest way to begin your marketing efforts. Your members will already have a relationship with your organization and trust will already be built, so it is a natural starting place. Other low cost effective ways to market your camp are to target local youth center directors, youth organizations, after school clubs, and middle school counselors. You can send them a letter along with some of your brochures asking them to share the information with any youth they feel might benefit from the camp. You can find their information online with a little searching and then enter their information into a spreadsheet that you can use when you are ready to market your camp.

 Campfire Wisdom: If there is a summer planner for parents in your local newspaper, it is usually free and is a great place to list your camp information. The deadline for postings is often in January, so make sure to check with your local newspaper early.

❒ **Check on insurance coverage**

You always want to minimize your risk as much as possible, which means you will want to make sure you obtain insurance coverage for the camp. There is usually a premium charged to the camp for insurance, so you will need to find out what the policy is and what it covers. I would recommend letting the parents know (we do it on our health form) that they should have their own existing health insurance coverage for their child because the camp insurance may not cover each and every scenario under the sun. If you are an organization, the Human Resources or Risk Management departments are usually who you would contact to find out this information.

Regardless, as a business owner inviting youth onto your property, any seasoned attorney or insurance agent will tell you that you have a high rate of exposure or liability. So take the time to meet with both legal counsel and insurance agents to confirm you have the appropriate type and amount of insurance to cover any type of foreseeable scenario. The small amount of diligence you put in on the front end can save you hours of worry if something were to occur.

Remember, planning is the time to consider all potential opportunities and outcomes. It is the time to put as many pieces in place to prepare for the exciting endeavor of training young entrepreneurs. Be part of the small group of us that over plans, considering each and every hazard and scenario to ensure you are in a position to sustain and move forward. Every step you take in the beginning may save you numerous steps in the end.

Three Months Before

After you focus and plan for the big pieces of the puzzle, you can then begin to shift your attention to the finite details that need to be addressed. These details are just as important as the big picture. If you are just three months out from the beginning of camp, you can probably feel the momentum building and the excitement mounting. By this time, you will have some campers registered and most likely have financially and physically prepared yourself for what's to come. Now it is time to dot the "i's" and cross the "t's."

❏   **Check inventory of supplies and watch for sales**

Having a list of supplies that are needed for the camp is very helpful. The list will allow you to see what you might already have on hand, watch for sales, and have time to get competitive bids for items that are being imprinted such as brief cases, t-shirts and water bottles. If you are using the More Than A Lemonade Stand™ name for your camp, you can order supplies directly from MoreThanALemonadeStand.com. Below is a complete list of supplies needed for the camp that you can use for a guideline.

 Campfire Wisdom: A great time to buy supplies for the camp is the back-to-school season when you can save a tremendous amount of money.

Consider the following sample camp supply list:

More Than a Lemonade Stand™
Camp Supply List (with options for less cost substitutes)

✓   Brief Case (imprinted with camp logo) – 1 per camper & leaders (Less Cost: Drawstring Back Pack)

✓   Name Tags with lanyards (this may be part of your registration system) 1 per camper & leaders

✓   Name Tents that campers can decorate – 1 per camper

✓   Three-Ring Binder with 3 binder tab dividers – 1 per camper & leaders

✓   Pad Folio with calculator & pen (or pens separately) – 1 per camper (Less Cost: notebook and pens)

- ✓ Laminated 'create your own' Luggage Tags - 2 per camper
- ✓ Inventor's Notebook – 1 per camper (optional section of camp)
- ✓ Magic Markers – 6 packages of 8 to 12 assorted colors
- ✓ Crayons – 6 packages of 24 assorted colors
- ✓ Digital Camera – to take pictures throughout the camp
- ✓ White Copier Paper – for printing camp materials – 4-5 reams
- ✓ Colored Copier Paper – 4 different colors – 1 ream of each color
- ✓ Legal Sheets folded like a tri-fold poster board to plan posters for their business idea (1-2 per camper)
- ✓ Scissors – will need at least 5 pairs for the business simulation (recommended 10 pairs)
- ✓ Thin Highlighter Markers – 1 box each of pink, green, and yellow
- ✓ T-shirts (imprinted with camp logo) – 1 per camper & leaders
- ✓ Avery 5371 Business Card Forms – approximately 2 sheets per camper
- ✓ 1 Roll of Butcher Paper (can also use white poster paper)
- ✓ White Poster Board – 8 sheets
- ✓ Lemonade Stand Supplies (budget $100 = $50 per team—dependent on what the teams decide and will need to be purchased after the camp begins)
- ✓ Tri-fold Poster Board (one per camper – have a few extra in case of mistakes)
- ✓ Bright Yellow Copier Paper for Ballots for Lemonade Stand

✓ Ballot Box for lemonade stand customers to vote on their favorite

✓ Award Certificates – 1 per camper

✓ Other things to give campers at ceremony (book, etc. - optional)

✓ Picture Slide Show (ready for ceremony)

✓ Beach Ball for game (or other game supplies-depending on what games are used)

✓ Jeopardy Game (optional)

✓ Business Simulation Materials (these are listed in the business simulation section)

❏ **Create a letter for targeted contacts/organizations**

Earlier in the planning process, you decided what organizations you were going to target for marketing and gathered contact information. You will want to start marketing your camp so you can make sure it fills by camp time. Parents register their kids for camps many months before the camp begins, so you will want to make sure they have the information when they are looking over their options. Registrations usually start coming into our camp six months before the camp commences, and it is usually full six to eight weeks prior to start.

To market to your contact list, you will need to create a cover letter or email to send along with the camp information. The purpose of the letter is for your contacts to share the information with students who they think would be interested in the camp. If you have scholarship information, it should be included along with the camp information.

Below is sample cover letter to use as a guideline:

More Than a Lemonade Stand ™
Youth Entrepreneur Camp 2014
Dates and Scholarship Information

Dear _____,

I'm excited to announce the 2014 dates for the More Than A Lemonade Stand ™ Youth Entrepreneur Camp for students currently in 6th, 7th or 8th grades. The dates and times for this commuter day camp are _____ and it will be held at _____. Please share the camp information with any students or teachers that might be interested in the camp *(NOTE: if sending to a youth organization change to students or parents)*. Enclosed are five brochures and scholarship information *(if applicable)*, if you need more copies of either, please contact me at the information below.

Scholarships are limited so please encourage students to apply as soon as possible. The camp usually fills up approximately 6 weeks before it begins, so please let them know to register early if they are interested in attending. Feel free to give me a call or email me if you have any questions.

Sincerely,
Julie Wood
Youth Entrepreneur Camp Director
More Than a Lemonade Stand™
Phone: *608-332-9836*
Email: *juliewood@eseedling.com*

❐ **Mail letter and camp information out**

Once the letter or email is completed, mail or email it to your contacts along with a packet of 5 brochures (or an attached brochure in the case of email) and the scholarship information so that they can share it with students or members.

❐ **Design T-shirts, water bottles, & brief cases**

Camps usually have "camp wear" to foster camp spirit; therefore it is a good idea to provide t-shirts, water bottles and brief cases for your camp. They should match your camp branding, so you will need to coordinate their design and color. You will also need to find a vendor. To make sure you get the best price, I would recommend getting three competitive bids to choose from. You will need to decide if you want to use your logo or other design, and decide if you want to come up with some type of slogan. Whatever you choose, make sure it will appeal to the kids or they will not want to wear or use the products (which is advertising for your camp). You could even have a t-shirt slogan contest during camp with the winner getting their slogan on the next year's shirts.

Campfire Wisdom: When the UW-Madison Youth Entrepreneur Camp was originally branded it had a brief case graphic on a white t-shirt and the kids didn't want to wear the shirts. A few years ago we came up with the slogan "We Mean Business," which we printed in white letters on red t-shirts (Wisconsin's colors) and the kids wore them multiple days during the camp, even during their team lemonade competition.

Two Months Before

As you begin to near the start of camp, now is the time to ensure you have all the supplies you need to execute your game plan. You will also begin building team rapport by getting to know your staff and allowing them the opportunity to offer feedback and be part of camp planning.

❒ **Order Supplies**

In order to make sure you have all your camp supplies on hand before the camp begins, you will want to check over what supplies you already have and then order the supplies that are on the detailed supply list that was included earlier in the planning section.

Many campsites will not be located in the big city, so be careful to ensure you have enough supplies to last you throughout the entire camp. If not, you may find yourself running around to secure extra pens, cardboard, or other necessities. There is no harm in over ordering, especially when you can use the leftovers for your next camp. But if you do find yourself running short on supplies, large companies like Amazon and Staples will be happy to deliver whatever you may need directly to your camp to prevent long trips to the big box stores.

❒ **Create business simulation or order the kit**

The business simulation is a major and important activity during the camp. When planning, there are two options: you can create it yourself with the procedures included in the curriculum section of the book, or you can order the complete

Biz Ops Game™ kit from www.morethanalemonadestand.com. In order to have it ready to go by camp time, you will want to assign someone to create the business simulation materials or order the kit at this time.

Make sure you do not overlook this integral piece of the camp, as it is not easily obtainable if you do. You'll find yourself working overtime to put it together if you have not already prepared it once camp begins.

❐ **Mail out direct mail promotional piece**
If your camp is not full (or close to being full) you will want to send your direct mail piece to your contact list. You could also send out an email blast if you don't have the budget, or if you did not create a promotional piece. You can use your member list, or another targeted list that you have.

You'll find the most traction amongst your first tier of contacts. Furthermore, target youth centers and schools, as they are the most likely markets for your camp. It is important to have enough campers enrolled so you can form multiple teams and keep the competition and the spirit at a high.

❐ **Complete background checks on staff**
You should always have a background check done on anyone that is working with youth. This is to minimize your risk with the staff you hire. If you didn't complete the background checks on staff when they were hired, you need to do it at this stage in the planning. You want to have this done early enough so that if something shows up from the check that wasn't anticipated, you can deal with it before the camp begins.

You can open yourself up to serious liability if you did not do a proper background check before hiring any employee. It is crucial to the safety and health of your campers that you hire qualified and morally competent staff members to run the show.

❐ Schedule a staff meeting to review schedule, roles, & content

Whenever you are working on a project that involves an entire team to be successful, the team should be involved in the actual implementation. This provides an opportunity for each of the team members to give his or her input and feel like he or she is an important part of the decisions being made. It will also allow for buy-in from the team members and it makes sure everyone is on the same page. The purpose of the meeting will be to review and discuss the schedule, content, guest speakers and field trip locations. This is also the time to clarify the roles of each team member and make assignments to each team member based on their strengths. At the end of the meeting, each team member will know what is expected of them and will be aware of deadlines and procedural guidelines.

I also subscribe to the notion that two heads are better than one. You never know what creative ideas team members will bring to the table to help elevate your camp and its curriculum. Open the meetings with a few minutes of going around the room, asking if anyone has any ideas or suggestions regarding topics that should be addressed, or activities that could be implemented.

One Month Before

Camp is right around the corner. By now, you should feel ready for your first camper to walk in the door. But there are still a few important steps to take to ensure your camp is well prepared for the exciting days to come.

❏ Email blast to list

If your camp isn't full, you can still get some additional attendees by sending out a promotional email to your list (or second email if you've already sent one out). In the subject line make sure to include a sense of urgency so they know to register today! Mail Chimp and Constant Contact are two online email programs that work well for promotions.

Start by sending a blast to your first level of connections, keeping it small to see what the response looks like. If that does not fit your needs, expand the list and continue on until you fill your camp.

❏ Complete CPR/First Aid certification

If you don't have at least one of your camp staff with a current CPR/First Aid certification, you will want to make sure that someone is certified before the camp begins. The American Red Cross and the American Heart Association both have certification courses. The certification is good for 2 years, so it is a good idea to train someone who will be there for two years.

The best practice is to ensure all counselors have attended and completed a CPR course to confirm all of your campers are safe and cared for by a professional and well-trained staff.

❒ Complete other required training

Some organizations require additional training on child protection. This is for your protection as much as it for the kids. Some organizations require that everyone who is a paid staff member complete the training every year. You will need to check with your particular organization to see if this is a requirement.

❒ Stock up on First Aid Kit

In case someone gets a cut, blister, or other minor injury, you will want to make sure you have a fully stocked first aid kit. Many organizations do not allow any type of medication or sunscreen to be given without parent permission, so in your health form you may want to include permission for the student to take Tylenol and self-apply cortisone cream or sunscreen, otherwise it is not allowed. Also, make sure you are aware of any medically related allergies so your staff is not dispensing medication to which a child may be allergic.

❒ Confirm guest speakers and businesses for field trip

The sample schedule included earlier in the book has several time slots for guest speakers and time for a field trip to local businesses. For the field trip, look at your area and see what businesses are close that may be interesting for the kids to visit. They seem to like food businesses and somewhat unique businesses the best. Then contact the business owner and see if they would be interested in having the camp visit. Usually

30-45 minutes works well; that way the kids can get a tour of the business and have a short time for questions.

We have tried five or six businesses for the field trip but it gets a little chaotic, so I would keep the number of businesses to four. For guest speakers, 30 minutes works well. Speakers should be energetic and have an interesting story, product, or service to discuss. Once the speakers and businesses are confirmed, you will want to make sure to update the camp schedule.

❐ **Confirm attendance and information with campers' guardians**

Sometimes plans change and busy families forget to let you know they are no longer interested, so it is a good idea to make sure everyone is going to attend the camp. This is especially important if the camp is full and there is a waiting list. It would be a shame to have someone on the waiting list not attend and then have a camper on the list not show up.

Always send an email to the parent or guardian to confirm that the camper is attending, also make sure to confirm that the email address is the one they want to use for camp correspondence. Take this opportunity to ask if there are any food allergies (if you are providing food) and remind them that payment is due before the camp. This is also a good time to confirm their mailing address and let them know camp forms will be mailed out soon. Another reason to email is that sometimes replies come back with questions about scholarships, so if you have scholarship funds still available they can complete an application before the camp begins.

❒ Create or update forms

Depending on what your organization already has on hand and what is required, you may need health forms to keep track of immunizations, food allergies, medications and any other medical information. Also important are the liability release and emergency contact form. This form releases you from liability for normal camp activities, notifies you of any medical conditions or food allergies that you need to deal with at camp, and gives you an emergency contact for the camper. Another form to consider if you want to use photos is a photo release form (for parents to sign). To make sure the campers do not think they can just come to the camp without any responsibilities, we include a ground rules form for parents and the camper to sign (this is included in the curriculum section). It is always advisable to have legal counsel review any forms that are used.

Below is a sample publicity release form:

Youth Entrepreneur Camp
Photo and Comments Release Form

I hereby grant permission to E-seedling, LLC to use photos and comments of my minor child, _____ _____, from the More Than a Lemonade Stand Youth Entrepreneur Camp for educational, informational and promotional purposes. I understand that these materials may be used for teacher training and may be posted on the Internet for a period of time.

Parent Name _____

Address _____

City, State, Zip _____

Phone _____

Parent Signature_____ Date _____

Below is a sample liability release and emergency contact form:

More Than A
Lemonade Stand™

Youth Entrepreneur Camp
Liability Release & Emergency Contact Form

I hereby give permission for my child, _____
_____, to participate in the Youth Entrepreneur Camp
under staff supervision, and agree to hold harmless E-seedling,
LLC and their employees from any and all liability, injury or
loss arising out of my child's participation in this program. I
certify that my child is fit to participate in all program activities.
In case of emergency, I grant permission for my child to be
given treatment at a local hospital.

Parent Signature_____Date_____
Please list any medical conditions, food allergies (and their
severity) or other information we should be aware of during
the camp:

_____
_____
_____

Emergency Contact information that can be reached during camp:
Name _____ Phone _____
Relationship _____

Campfire Wisdom: If you copy the forms on different colored paper it is much easier to keep track of which forms you have for each camper when they get mailed back to you.

❒ **Create a parent memo to send with camp forms and information**

Many parents are nervous about sending their kids to camp. To alleviate some of their anxiety, I send a memo with detailed camp information so they can feel more confident and be informed. The memo also includes information about what forms need to be completed and the awards ceremony that they are invited to attend. Parents appreciate the communication and information and it helps them feel more comfortable about sending their child to camp.

Below is a sample parent memo:

TO: Youth Entrepreneur Camp Parents/Guardians
FROM: Julie Wood, Director
More Than a Lemonade Stand Youth Entrepreneur Camp
DATE: (date)
RE: Camp Information and Forms

Enclosed are the forms we need completed in order for your child to attend the Youth Entrepreneur Camp held (include dates) at (location) from (times). Please make arrangements to pick up your camper by (time) at the entrance of the school. It is extremely important that our camp staff knows if arrangements are made other than pick up at (time) each day of camp.

On **Friday (date)**, we have an **awards ceremony and poster presentation at (time) which you are encouraged to attend.** Also enclosed is a short introductory letter for the camp participant.

Please complete the enclosed forms listed below and return them in the prepaid postage envelope by (date). If you cannot get them in the mail by then, please bring the completed forms when you sign in on the first day of camp, (date). Check-in is from (time) the first day of camp and no camper will be allowed to participate without completed and signed forms.

- Liability Release & Emergency Contact Form
- Permission to Use Release Form
- Health Form (please complete both sides of form)
- Ground Rules, Expectations & Consequences (both guardian and camper must sign)

If your son or daughter has any food allergies or special dietary requirements please call me at _____ by (date) so that meal arrangements can be made.

Even though this is a fun interactive camp, we expect the participants to come with respect for the instructors and peers and have a willingness to learn and participate in the activities. If respect and courtesy are not exhibited at the camp, we reserve the right to send the camper home.

If you have any questions regarding these forms, please call me at _____.

We look forward to a fun week!

❐ **Create a camper memo with camp information**

To start building rapport with the campers and to model how to communicate within a business format, I send a camper memo along with the parent memo and camp information. This alleviates some of their anxiety about camp by letting them know what they will be doing during the week. It also gives them time to think about a business idea to work on during camp.

Below is a sample camper memo:

TO: Youth Entrepreneur Camp **Participant**
FROM: Julie Wood, Director
More Than a Lemonade Stand Youth Entrepreneur Camp
DATE: (include date)
RE: Introduction to Youth Entrepreneur Camp Week

We are excited for your participation in the upcoming Youth Entrepreneur Camp on (dates, time and location). We have many fun activities including:

- A Business Simulation where you create and sell products
- Computer projects including creating your own business cards and a business presentation
- Fun games
- Guest Speakers and Field trips to area businesses
- A Team Lemonade Stand Competition

If you could start thinking about some business ideas that you would like to work on during the camp as your individual project that would be great. If you already have one, that's even better! Also, think about any graphics or pictures you might like to use on the business card you will make to promote your new business!

Even though this is a fun interactive camp, we expect you to show respect for the instructors and your peers. If you do not exhibit these behaviors you may be sent home. Please make sure to read the expectations document and sign it along with your parent or guardian.

Again, we look forward to working with you at the upcoming camp. If you have any questions please feel free to call me at (include number).

See you at camp!

❐ **Mail forms and letters to parents and camper**

Once all the forms along with the parent and camper letter(s) are ready, they should get mailed as a packet of information. To make it as easy as possible for parents to return the forms, include a self-addressed stamped envelope to your preferred address and make sure you include a due date of a week before the camp starts so that you have ample time to organize.

This will help to ensure each of your campers has the appropriate forms sent in before camp begins. Otherwise, you'll find yourself spending a lot of time on registration during drop-off day confirming that each camper's paperwork is in good working order.

Campfire Wisdom: The first day of camp goes much smoother if you send the forms out ahead of time and ask for them to be returned 1 week before camp. Be sure to include a return stamped envelope. That way the first day of camp can be used answering parents' questions and verifying the health information instead of checking in all of the forms and making sure they are complete.

❑ **Review curriculum & videos used and update if needed**

If you haven't reviewed and updated the curriculum yet, you will want to do it now so that you can make sure you are familiar and ready to teach it to the campers. It is also a good idea to check any video links that you have included in your materials to make sure they are still current. If any video links have changed, you will need to update them or find a new video for the content you are teaching. If any new curriculum is being developed, it should be assigned to a staff member with a due date that will give you plenty of time to copy the information (at least one week before the camp begins) and get the curriculum ready for the camp.

❑ **Order Food**

You should have decided when you were budgeting for your camp whether or not you were going to include food. You should have food allergy information from emailing the parents and you will need to keep that information in mind when ordering food.

From experience, I have found that a light breakfast such as fruit, granola, yogurt, milk and water (no high sugar items) works well and can also be used as morning snacks. Most kids tend to eat breakfast before coming to camp, but sometimes need a mid-morning snack. Lunch depends on your budget and what is available at your venue. I have found that the kids like a mixture of 'do it yourself' sandwiches, 'do it yourself' nacho and taco bar, pasta bars, and pizza.

Afternoon snacks are nice, but not a must. If you have an afternoon walking field trip scheduled and there is some place to get ice cream or other snack such as popcorn that works great. If there is a large enough lunch then snacks are not really necessary.

You must provide water pitchers and cups (or water bottles) so that the kids can always remain hydrated. You will find budgeting and prepping for meals to be one of the hardest parts of creating a successful camp. It can be one of your largest expenses and should never be approximated. If you have little training in the food industry, make sure you do your research or hire a professional to help you budget and plan meals accordingly. If you simply guesstimate what these costs may be, you could literally give away all of your profit from the camp.

Two Weeks Before Camp

By this time, you are literally days away from your first campers entering the door. But these last minute preparatory steps can be the difference between running a good camp and a great one. Addressing issues like transportation, forms, and finalizing a schedule will be an important part of your ability to run a seamless camp.

❐ Reserve Bus for Field Trip

If you are going to have a field trip day that is not within walking distance, then you will need to reserve a bus for your field trip. If you are at a school, they may already have transportation services that you can use. Otherwise, there are usually local bus drivers who are independent operators and provide bus service to groups for a fee. They should already have insurance that will cover the campers, but be sure to check with the transportation company just to be safe.

❐ Prepare Check-off Sheet for Forms

To keep track of who has sent their forms back, create a check-off sheet for when forms are returned to you (from the parent letter above). That way you can remind the parents who haven't sent the forms back yet.

Below is a sample check-off sheet:

Forms Check-off

Camper Name	Health Form	Liability Release Form	Photo Release Form	Ground Rules

Campfire Wisdom: Before printing out the form, type in the campers' names in alphabetical order – this will make it faster when keeping track of the completed forms. Then file the forms in alphabetical order by campers' name so you can find them quickly if needed.

❏ **Create an injury report form**

Some organizations and insurance companies require an injury report when a camper is injured. The report is a description of what happened, how it happened, and what was done for the injury. Create a form to use that includes the name of the camper, the date and time, the location, a description of what happened, and what was done. You may want to check with your organization as they may have a required form and a required person to file it with.

❏ **Finalize schedule and materials**

The schedule will need to be finalized when all of the speakers and field trips are confirmed so that it can be updated and copied. This is your communication tool for staff and parents. On the first morning of camp you may want to give parents a schedule when they drop off their camper. It helps put the parents' minds at ease to see what the kids will be doing each day.

Campfire Wisdom: If you put a schedule in the camper binder (which is recommended), leave the times off—the kids get preoccupied with the times and if they are not exact, they will certainly let you know!

❐ **Get materials copied**

The materials need to be copied so that they can be assembled in time for camp. This can be done in-house if you have the resources, or sent to a copy shop for copying. Make sure you create more than enough packets for your campers and staff. Assume that many will be lost and/or destroyed in the excitement. It is a lot easier to have a few extra to be used for the next camp rather than having to find print-on-demands or copy machines at the local grocery or drug store. Make sure the packets are stapled together or put in a binder and are easy to read and understand.

One Week Before

By this time, you should be able to take a few deep breaths since the majority of the planning is behind you. You should feel at ease and ready for the campers to arrive. However, don't pat yourself on the back just yet. Now is the time to make any final adjustments and double check all of your work and planning. Once you get inside of a week, you will begin to run out of time if you need to make any material alterations to the plan or schedule.

❐ **Final preparation of materials**

Once all the materials are copied, they can be assembled and organized for the camp. Three ring binders work well to create a camp workbook for the kids. Tab dividers can be used to divide the sections. Office supply stores sell printable tab dividers that you can use to create your own custom tabs—this will keep the cost lower than having tabs preprinted. Colored paper works well to keep each subject that is being taught separate and easily accessible during the camp (more about the different subjects and handouts in the curriculum section).

❑ Check-off forms as they come in

To save time, as soon as you start receiving the forms back from the parents, you should review them to make sure there is no missing information. If complete, check them off on the check-off sheet you created earlier. If there is any missing information, you can note it on the check-in sheet so you know what is needed the first morning of camp. The check-off sheet is very helpful the first morning of camp (when it can be a little chaotic) so that you can be efficient about what still needs to be collected.

❑ Organize materials by day

You will want to organize the materials before the camp begins so you are ready for when the campers arrive. I have found that the Friday before camp is a great day to get organized; that way you aren't worrying about everything the weekend before camp. Organizing the materials by day seems to be the most efficient way of organizing the materials; I usually create boxes with each day on them and then put all of the materials for that day in the box. If you have room to store the materials in the location where the camp is being held, it is the easiest so that you don't have to haul supplies and materials back and forth. If you don't have room in the location of the camp then you can load them on a cart to make it easier to move the materials.

By now, you are ready to go. Your camp is prepped, your campers are enrolled and excited to board the bus on day one, and you should be ready to execute your months of preparation. Take the last twenty-four hours to review your checklist one final time, and then have a nice meal, get a good night's rest, and wake up bright eyed and ready to welcome your campers face to face.

To recap all of the previously mentioned prep, take a look at a checklist summary of all the tasks mentioned above:

More than a Lemonade Stand
Camp Planning and Implementation Checklist

Six Months Before Camp

Name your camp and create a logo

Choose and reserve a Venue

Create a budget and price your camp

Find sponsors

Staff your camp

Create a brochure/promotional piece

Create a website or update page on existing site

Decide on number and dollar amount of scholarships

Decide on who marketing to & gather contact information

Check on Insurance coverage to see if sufficient

Three Months Before Camp

Check Inventory of supplies & watch for sales

Create letter for organizations' marketing to

Mail camp information to organizations' marketing to

Design T-shirts, water bottles & brief cases

Two Months Before Camp

Order pad folios (1 per camper)

Order brief cases (1 per camper)

Order laminated plain luggage tags (2 per camper)

Order Printable Business Cards (Avery 5371 compatible)

Order Display Boards for Poster Session (1 per camper)

Order Poster paper for Lemonade Stand (10 sheets total)

Order T-shirts (1 per camper & staff)

Order Water Bottles (1 per camper & staff)

Order paper, markers, scissors & general office supplies

Order Lanyard Style Name Tags

Order or Make Name Tents

Create business simulation or order Biz Ops Game™

Mail out direct mail promotional piece

Complete background checks on staff (if haven't already)

Schedule staff meeting to review schedule, roles & content

One Month Before Camp

Promotional email blast to list (if camp isn't full)

Complete CPR/First Aid certification

Complete other required training

Stock up on First Aid Kit

Confirm Businesses for Field Trips

Contact & Confirm guest speakers

Create or update photo release form

Create or update liability release form

Create or update health information form

Create a parent memo with camp information

Create a camper memo with camp information

Mail forms & letters to parents and camper

Review curriculum & update if needed

Review videos used and update if needed

Order Food and make sure room(s) set up is finalized

Two Weeks Before Camp

Reserve Bus for Field Trip

Prep Check-off Sheet for forms

Create an injury report form

Finalize Schedule and Materials

Get Materials copied

One Week Before Camp

Final preparation of materials

Check-off Forms as they come in

Organize materials by day

Section II

Camp Curriculum:
And Now the Fun Begins:
||||||||||||||||||||||||||||||||||||||||||||||||||||||||||||||||||||

I am sure you feel as if it has been a long road to get to this point. Look around—there are actual campers beginning to board the bus and drive towards you and your camp! Months ago you started the process of planning for this day and it is finally here. With that said, it is time to really embrace all of your hard work and enjoy all that your camp has to offer. You will find that you'll probably enjoy the experience as much as your campers do, and my guess is that you will learn an enormous amount from them as well.

So with that said, here we go…

Overview/Schedule

There are five main activities that are completed by the kids during the camp:

1) Development of individual business ideas that includes a 3-minute presentation to the campers and counselors;

2) Development of their business idea poster with a presentation for family and friends;

3) Development of their own business card;

4) The large Team Lemonade Stand Competition; and

5) The small group Biz Ops Game™ business simulation.

The camp also includes walking field trips, a bus field trip, guest speakers, and additional team and individual learning activities. We have found that this mix of activities gives the campers a great variety and allows them to learn the basics of entrepreneurship (along with how to start and run a business) in a fun and engaging manner.

Below are two options for camp curriculum overall schedules:

The first is a one-week program where campers attend camp for full days (9am – 4 pm) Monday-Friday.

The second is a half-day, two week (1pm-4pm) Monday-Friday option that could be done as a summer school. The second option has the three-minute individual business presentations taken out to accommodate for the shorter time periods each day. These schedules can be adapted based on the schedule you have for your own camp or program.

Each of the activities included in the schedules will be described in more detail so that you can utilize them in your own camp or program. I'm including the schedules to use as a guide for timing and mixture of activities. Even though these schedules are proven, you may have other activities you want to include. Feel free to adapt the schedules so that they best benefit your camp. With that said, let's take a look at the first option for your More Than a Lemonade Stand youth entrepreneurship camp:

<u>**Option 1**</u>
More Than a Lemonade Stand™
Youth Entrepreneur Camp
Five-Day Camp Plan
9:00 a.m. - 4:00 p.m.; Lunch & Snacks provided

<u>**Monday**</u>

9:00 am – 10:30 am	**Forms check-in; Double-check Health Forms**
	Pretest –What do you know about being an Entrepreneur?
	Make Luggage Tags for brief cases (after finish pre-test)
	Group Name Game
	Ground Rules, Discipline and Consequences
	Overview of the week
10:30 am – 10:40 am	**Break**
10:45 am – 12:15 pm	**Biz Ops Game™**
12:15 p.m. – 12:45 pm	**Lunch**
12:45-pm – 2:15 pm	**Define Your Own Business Idea – (golden rod) (15 mins)**

	Break out into small Departmental Groups (60 mins – 15 min/dept)
	1. **Marketing and Sales**- (Blue)
	2. **Accounting and Finance**- (Green)
	3. **Creating a Product or Service**- (Purple)
	4. **Customer Service**- (Pink)
2:15 pm – 3:55 pm	**Walking Field Trip & Ice Cream Break**
3:55 pm – 4:00 pm	**Gather Materials/Name Tags and exit as group for Pickup**

Tuesday

9:00 am – 9:30 am	**Beach Ball Game**
9:30 am – 10:00 am	**Guest Speaker**
10:00 am – 10:15 am	**Break**
10:15 am – 11:15 am	**Work in Departments (same as Monday – 15 mins/dept)**
11:15 am – 12:00 pm	**Start Posters for Businesses**
12:00 pm – 12:30 pm	**Lunch**
12:30 pm – 12:45 pm	**Professionalism**
12:45 pm - 2:15 pm	**Computer Lab**
	• Design Business Cards
	• Work on business plan PowerPoint presentations (3 min presentation)
	• Work on posters (if time permits)
2:15 pm – 2:30 pm	**Break**

2:30 pm – 4:00 pm	**Teams Work on Lemonade Stand (yellow)**

- Show lemonade stand videos
- Team Activity: birthdates
- Number off for teams
- Work in Teams: pick a company name, theme, color, and Shopping List

Wednesday

9:00 am – 12:30 pm	**Bus Field trip to local small businesses**
12:30pm - 1:00 pm	**Lunch**
1:00 pm – 2:15 pm	**Debrief Field Trip** Characteristics of an Entrepreneur (Poster drawings)
2:15 pm – 2:45 pm	**Business Ethics – Identity & Reputation**
2:45 pm – 3:00 pm	**Break**
3:00 pm – 4:00 pm	**Teams Work on Lemonade Stand preparation**

Thursday

9:00 am - 9:30 am	**Guest Entrepreneur Speaker**
9:30 am – 10:00 am	**Presentation Skills**
10:00 am- 10:15 am	**Break**
10:15 am – 11:00 am	**Computer Lab** Finish business plan PowerPoint presentations

	When finished, work on posters
11:00 am – 11:45 am	**Final Prep for Lemonade Stand**
11:45 am – 12:15 pm	**Lunch**
12:30 pm - 1:45 pm	**Set up, Sell & Clean up Lemonade Stand**
1:45 pm – 2:15 pm	**Debrief Lemonade stand**
2:15 pm – 2:30 pm	**Break**
2:30 pm - 3:00 pm	**Guest Speaker**
3:00 pm - 4:00 pm	**Work on Thank You Cards & Business Posters**

Friday

9:00 am – 9:30 am	**Post Test and Evaluations**
9:30 am - 11:30 am	**Business Plan Presentations –** 3 minutes each
10:15 am – 10:30 am	**Break – take break ½ through presentations**
11:45 am - 1:00 pm	**Lunch**
1:00 pm – 2:30 pm	**Biz Ops Game™**
2:30 pm – 3:00 pm	**Get room ready for Award Ceremony**
3:00 pm - 4:00 pm	**Award Ceremony & Poster Session – Families invited** Certificates, Picture & Book Closing Comments

If you are considering a longer running camp, or feel your students would be better served by shorter and more focused days, the following option may be a better fit. Option 2 consists of a ten-day camp with students attending camp for a period of three hours each day. That is four hours less than Option 1 and is a better fit for younger campers or those that should decide to split their days between multiple camps. In addition to considering the age of your potential campers, survey your overall goals, the portion of the summer you are holding the camp (beginning v. end), and your speaker and field trip availability. Each of those aspects will help you to decide which Option will better fit you and your campers. Initially, if you feel that a longer camp with shorter days is the right fit, consider the following schedule and curriculum:

<u>Option 2</u>
More Than a Lemonade Stand
Youth Entrepreneur Camp
Ten-Day Camp Plan; 3 hours each day

Week 1:
Monday

1:00 pm – 2:15 pm	**Check-in and Group Game**
	Pretest – What do you know about being an Entrepreneur?
	Handout Supplies
	Ground Rules, Discipline and Consequences
	Overview of the camp
	Introductions - Game
2:15 pm – 2:30 pm	**Break – Kids should bring their own snacks**

2:30 pm – 4:00 pm	**Biz Ops Game**™

Tuesday

1:00-pm – 2:30 pm	**Define Your Own Business Idea**
	Small Business Basics- Break-out in small groups
	1) Accounting and Finance
	2) Marketing and Sales
2:30 p.m. – 2:45 pm	**Break – Kids should bring their own snacks**
2:45 pm – 4:00 pm	**Walking Tour – to local area businesses**

Wednesday

1:00 pm – 2:15 pm	**Beach Ball Game**
2:15 pm – 2:45 pm	**Story of an Entrepreneur – Guest Speaker**
2:45 pm – 3:00 pm	**Break – Kids should bring their own snacks**
3:00 pm– 4:00 pm	**Small Business Basics- Break-out in small groups**
	3) Creating a Product or Service
	4) Customer Service

Thursday

1:00 pm – 1:30 pm	**Business Name worksheet**
1:30 pm – 2:45 pm	**Computer Lab**
	• Design Business Cards

	• Work on business plan presentations
2:45 pm – 3:00 pm	**Break – Kids should bring their own snacks**
3:00 pm – 4:00 pm	**Walking field trip to local area business**

Friday

1:00 pm – 2:00 pm	**Work on 3 questions for field trip Start planning posters**
2:00 pm – 2:15 pm	**Line up by birthdates- for Lemonade Stand Teams**
2:15 pm – 2:30 pm	**Break – Kids should bring their own snacks**
2:30 pm – 3:50 pm	**Teams Work on Lemonade Stand**
	• Show lemonade stand videos
	• Work in Teams: pick a company name, theme, colors
3:50 pm – 4:00 pm	**Hand out t-shirts to wear on field trip on Monday**

Week 2:
Monday

1:00 pm – 3:30 pm	**Walking Field trip to local small businesses** (15 min break sometime during field trip)
3:30pm – 4:00 pm	**Take group picture on field trip or upon return**

Tuesday

1:00 pm – 1:15 pm	**Debrief Field Trip** (small groups – each take 1 business)
1:15 pm – 1:30 pm	**Large Group - Share finding from small groups**
1:30 pm – 2:00 pm	**Characteristics of an Entrepreneur (Poster drawings - 4 groups)**
2:00 pm – 2:30 pm	**Business Ethics, Identity & Reputation, Professionalism**
2:30 pm – 2:45 pm	**Break – Kids should bring their own snacks**
2:45 pm – 4:00 pm	**Teams Work on Lemonade Stand Preparation-Need Shopping List**

Wednesday

1:00 pm – 2:30 pm	**Computer Lab** Finish Business plans; work on posters
2:30 pm – 2:45 pm	**Break – Kids should bring their own snacks**
2:45 pm – 4:00 pm	**Final Prep for Lemonade Stand**

Thursday

1:00 pm – 2:30 pm	**Set up, Sell & Clean up Lemonade Stand**
2:30 pm – 2:45 pm	**Break – Kids should bring their own snacks**
2:45 pm – 3:15 pm	**Debrief Lemonade Stand**

| 3:15 pm – 3:45 pm | **Work on Thank You Cards & Business Posters** |
| 3:45 pm – 4:00 pm | **What did I Learn?** - Post Test and evaluations |

Friday

1:00 pm – 2:30 pm	**Biz Ops Game**™
2:30 pm – 2:45 pm	**Get room ready for Award Ceremony**
2:45 pm – 3:00 pm	**Break – Networking with other campers**
3:00 pm - 4:00 p.m.	**Award Ceremony & Poster Session – Families invited**

First Day of Camp

Once you are all prepped and ready to go, you will quickly come face to face with the exciting opportunity of beginning your camp. The first day of camp is an amazing occasion to make fantastic first impressions. However, it can be somewhat overwhelming with the kids coming in at different times, parents asking questions, and on top of that dealing with all the forms; therefore, it is important that you have a plan of outlining who is designated with each responsibility. With that in mind, consider the following list of important tasks to designate to your staff as the buses start rolling in:

❐ **Forms Check-in; Double-check Health Forms, Answer Questions, Greet the Campers with a Handshake**

The three most important things when the campers arrive are:

1) All forms must be accounted for.

2) That the health form is verified by a parent/guardian. (From the letter sent earlier in the planning section— the parent/guardian should know that they should be with their camper the first morning.) This is to make sure you are covered in all aspects possible in case of emergency. You will want to make sure there is one staff person double-checking to see that all the forms are in and to verify the health form.

3) Drop off and pick up instructions for each camper are confirmed with the camper's parent or guardian.

After that the most important thing is to make sure both the camper and parent/guardian are comfortable with the camp situation. You will want to make sure you have a staff member available to answer parent and camper questions as they arrive.

The next thing to do at the camp is have one person (usually the director) greet the campers with a firm business handshake. This sets the tone for the camp as a business camp and starts the relationship building for the week. It is also the first teaching moment since many kids don't know how to give a firm handshake. Over the course of the camp, it's something that is worked on as a group, and campers are congratulated once they get it.

❒ **Pretest –What do you know about being an Entrepreneur? And Self-Perceptions**

After the camper is greeted, there are a few different tasks to be completed. First of all, if you are measuring outcomes, you will want to give them a pretest to complete. Below is a sample pretest that can be used at your camp. Since the camp teaches not only business skills, but also leadership skills it is a good idea to measure both business skills and self-perception since that is something that will improve during the camp.

More Than a Lemonade Stand Survey pg 1					
Part 1 - Personal Opinion (there is no right or wrong answer)					
Please circle the answer that best describes your opinion.	**Strongly Agree**	**Agree**	**Neutral**	**Disagree**	**Strongly Disagree**
1. I plan on owning my own business.	5	4	3	2	1
2. After high school, I plan to continue my education.	5	4	3	2	1
3. I am willing to learn the skills and knowledge needed to get a good job.	5	4	3	2	1
4. I am willing to study hard to get into the college of my choice.	5	4	3	2	1
5. I know enough to start a business and be successful.	5	4	3	2	1
6. Graduating from high school is important to me.	5	4	3	2	1
7. Giving back to my community is important to me.	5	4	3	2	1
8. I have the ability to control my own future.	5	4	3	2	1
9. Saving money is important to me.	5	4	3	2	1
10. I want to be a leader in my community.	5	4	3	2	1

11. Being honest & fair is important in doing business.	5	4	3	2	1
12. My unique gifts and talents can help me succeed in business.	5	4	3	2	1
13. Setting measurable goals will help me achieve them.	5	4	3	2	1
14. Taking responsibility for my actions is important.	5	4	3	2	1
15. Having a positive attitude will help me succeed in life.	5	4	3	2	1
16. Having skills & ability to financially support myself is important.	5	4	3	2	1
17. I feel good about myself.	5	4	3	2	1
18. There is no limit on what I can achieve if I put my mind to it.	5	4	3	2	1
19. I can make a difference in the world.	5	4	3	2	1
20. I can use my unique gifts and talents to help others.	5	4	3	2	1

More Than a Lemonade Stand Survey pg 2				
Part II - Measures your current business knowledge. Please circle the letter for the answer that is the most correct.				
1. A person who buys something from a business is a:	A. Employer	B. Retailer	C. Customer	D. I don't know
2. Business expenses that are the same each month are:	A. Expense Accounts	B. Fixed Costs	C. Variable Costs	D. I don't know
3. Every business sells:	A. Food/clothes	B. Merchandise	C. Products and/or services	D. I don't know
4. The money needed to start a business is:	A. Operating Expense	B. Startup Costs	C. Cost of Goods	D. I don't know
5. A written document that describes what your business is and how you operate it is:	A. A marketing plan	B. A Business plan	C. A budget	D. I don't know
6. What is an entrepreneur?	A. A side dish at a French café	B. A person who interprets foreign language	C. Someone who starts a business	D. I don't know
7. Money that comes into a business when a product or service is sold.	A. Profit	B. Petty Cash	C. Income or Revenue	D. I don't know
8. The 3 best ways to advertise a Youth-owned business is:	A. TV, Radio & Newspaper	B. Malls, Walmart & Shopko	C. Signs, Flyers & Business Cards	D. I don't know

9. If you are not taking care of your customers who will?	A. Your parents	B. Your competition	C. Your teachers	D. I don't know
10. A Green Business	A. Is a bad idea	B. Good for the environment	C. Sells green products	D. I don't know
11. When you subtract expenses from income you get:	A. Cost of Goods Sold	B. Profit	C. Capital Gain	D. I don't know
12. Rivalry between businesses to get the same customers is called:	A. Cheating	B. Competition	C. Scarcity	D. I don't know
13. Target customers refers to:	A. People who may need your product or service	B. People with lots of money	C. People who like archery	D. I don't know
14. In business, marketing is:	A. Telling people about your business.	B. Investing in the Stock market	C. Going to the farmer's market.	D. I don't know
15. If you sell a product for $5 and the cost is $1 then which statement is true?	A. The profit is $4	B. The hidden costs are $4	C. The revenue is $4	D. I don't know
16. The "bottom line" for a business is:	A. Capital Gain	B. Profit/(Loss)	C. Overhead	D. I don't know
17. A person who invests money in another person's business is:	A. Banker	B. Mentor	C. Angel Investor	D. I don't know

18. "Bootstrapping" is:	A. Dressing up for a business meeting.	B. Being hard to work for.	C. Starting small and working hard to succeed.	D. I don't know
19. If you make your customers unhappy who will they tell?	A. Their Friends	B. Their family	C. Both A and B	D. I don't know
20. Who is responsible for customer service?	A. Everyone who works at the business	B. Only the salesperson	C. Only the Owner	D. I don't know

❐   **Create Luggage Tags and Name Tents**

Once campers have their pretest completed and handed in, they can come get a luggage tag to decorate and attach to their brief case. This is so they know which one is theirs since they all look alike and can easily get mixed up. If you get laminated ones, it is a good idea to have a staff member help with the lamination and attaching to the brief case. The next thing is to have them decorate a name tent with their first name and a graphic that helps identify them (an interest, hobby, their business idea, etc.). This makes it easier and faster to learn their names. The kids will finish these at different times, so they can look over their materials while they are waiting.

❐   **Getting to Know Each Other Game**

Once everyone is checked in and done with their initial activities, it's a good time for an ice- breaker. There are many team activities built into the camp, so it is a good idea for the kids and staff to get to know each other as soon as possible. Games and activities are great for learning each other's names.

One game that we have used is called the name game. Everyone stands in a big circle and the starting person says a word that starts with the same letter as their first name followed by their first name (example: Jumping Julie). The next person says the one before them and then their own (example: Jumping Julie, Munching Michelle) and so on until the last person says everyone before them and then their own. This game can take some time so if you are running late on time; I would recommend the kids do a shortened version of this game by just using the names and not adding a label.

Another game that works well is the group resume. Teams of kids (I would suggest each table) create a resume of the skills and experience of their team. They could come up with a team name and then list years of education, years of lessons, activities, teams, etc. This will allow the kids to get to know each other in their team, start working together right away, and realize that they each have unique gifts, talents and knowledge that they bring to the camp. If you wanted to give an example, you could have the camp staff members create their own team resume to show before the kids start the activity.

 Campfire Wisdom: At the beginning of the camp the kids are quiet; don't be alarmed. This is normal and you should cherish it since it won't be quiet for long.

❏ **Ground Rules, Discipline and Consequences Review and Additions**

Even though the rules were already included in the pre-camp materials and signed by both the camper and a parent, it is a good idea to go over the expectations to make sure everyone is on the same page. After they are discussed as a group, it is a good time to ask for the campers' feedback on any additional ground rules they think would be good to add. The staff member who is facilitating the discussion can list them on a flipchart. This will help the kids feel they have a part in determining the rules for the week and it gives them practice with teamwork. The kids can then add them on their own ground rules sheet in their binders. Below is an example of the ground rules, expectations and consequences.

Basic Ground Rules:

- Be on time each day and make sure someone is here to pick you up at 4:00 each day.
- Respect the other campers and their contributions, even when you disagree.
- Laugh <u>with</u> others—not at others.
- Be responsible for your materials.
- All participants should contribute to discussions because all contributions are important.
- Listen while others are talking.
- Respect and show courteous behavior towards each other and the instructors.

Please note any additional rules agreed upon during our camp discussion:

Expectations:
- Share your strengths and talents with fellow campers.
- Make new friends.
- Learn to use the Internet as a learning resource.
- Learn more about using PowerPoint or Prezi to make professional presentations.
- Learn from other people's experiences.
- Learn what it takes to start your own business.
- Create your own business poster for family and friends.
- Create a presentation and present it to the class.
- Create your own business card for your business idea.

Please note any additional expectations agreed upon during our camp discussion:

Consequences:
- If you do not follow the ground rules and expectations you will receive a warning from one of the camp instructors.
- If you are warned 3 times you will be escorted to the office and your parent/guardian will be notified.
- If the behavior continues you will have to leave the camp.

❐ Overview of the Week

After the ground rules are established, the kids are anxious to know what they are going to be doing for the week. They want to know how it all fits together and the different projects that they will be working on. This is last part of the introduction to camp section and it provides the overview for the week. This can be done using a Prezi or a PowerPoint presentation. Below is an outline you can use for your presentation.

- 3 Big Things
    1. Have Fun
    2. Team Lemonade Stand
    3. Individual Business Presentation
- Have Fun
    1. Make new friends
    2. Field Trips
    3. Business Simulations
    4. Learning
- Team Lemonade Stand
    1. Work as a team to have a successful Lemonade Stand business
    2. Earn Money for the Youth Entrepreneur Camp Scholarship Fund
    3. Compete with other teams for best customer service, best tasting, best team work, and overall profit
- Your Own Business Idea
    1. Find a Business Idea that you can work on
    2. Create a business card

3. Work on Marketing, Accounting, Customer Service and Operations for your product or service
4. Present your business on Friday
5. Create a poster for closing ceremony; invite your family and friends

❒ **Break(s)**

The kids can't sit still too long and research has proven that your brain works best in 90-minute intervals, so breaks should be given approximately every 90 minutes or so. Be sure to emphasize that this is the time to use the restroom so they don't ask right after break and miss any of the camp activities.

Sometimes, offering your campers the ability to run around and maybe play a few games of dodge ball or capture the flag can really refresh their minds and keep them focused on their tasks. Have them go outside and get a few breaths of fresh air as well.

 Campfire Wisdom: Whenever you go to a different location (whether it be a different room or a field trip—walking or otherwise) it takes time to count the kids to make sure everyone in the group is accounted for. To make it easier, assign each adult camp counselor a specific group of kids. That way you don't have to count the entire group every time you move from place to place. It also a good idea to use the buddy system when going on walking or bus field trips.

Section III

Executing the Plan: Building Memories

||||||||||||||||||||||||||||||||||||||||||||||||||||||||

Just as you quickly break the ice for your new campers, you'll find yourself ready to dive head first into your camp curriculum. Executing your game plan is imperative to building a strong camp experience. Your curriculum is truly the lifeblood and the heart and soul of your camp. It is what will fill your camper's days and keep them interested and intrigued in the overall experience. It will provide them with a monumental learning opportunity that can plant the seed of entrepreneurship that will grow through the years and begin to burn like a fire that cannot be extinguished. Your curriculum should be approachable and understandable, uplifting and exciting, unique and interesting.

With that said, let's spend some time focusing on the integral parts of your curriculum.

Biz Ops Game ™

The most fundamental part of any Lemonade Stand curriculum is The Biz Ops Game™. The Biz Ops Game™ is a fun and engaging business simulation that teaches campers the basics of the day-to-day operations of running a manufacturing and retail business. It teaches creativity, teamwork, business roles and responsibilities, wholesale distribution, purchasing, financial recordkeeping, sales, customer service, manufacturing and quality control in approximately 90 minutes.

The concept of the game is based on teams (of 4 or 5 members) that are running an airplane company where they manufacture, test, and sell paper airplanes. As the activity is introduced and described, the teams start out by coming up with a name for their company and assigning each person a role based on their individual strengths. They then proceed through the normal business day by creating paper airplanes and then decorating them based on the customer theme for that day. The sales person must then demonstrate the airplane and sell it to the customer (played by a staff member). To keep things lively, the customer makes specific requests of the sales person who then must share with their team so that they can complete it during the next day of operations (each day is approximately 10-15 minutes). At the end of the week, dollar sales, quantity sales and net profit are calculated to determine the winner.

Teaching business operations in this experiential learning platform brings the kids right into the everyday operations of running a business so they can experience it firsthand. It gives them an idea of what is necessary to keep a business running and make a profit. It gives them the base they need for developing their own ideas into a viable business. It also gives them the base they need for learning more about business concepts, their own strengths, and working in a team environment.

Here are the instructions for creating and running the Biz Ops Game™.

Time Needed: Allow 90 minutes to complete the simulation and debriefing.

Supplies Needed:

Scissors – minimum of one pair of scissors per four to five person team.

Play money – can copy and cutout, or pull from an old game that has play money. You may also be able to purchase some at your local dollar store (there are also some websites that have printable play money). You need money to pay the salesperson when selling their product and for giving change when the teams buy raw materials at the office supply store. Suggested amounts to have: $500=40, $100=50, $50=50, $20=100, and $10=50.

Colored markers – if you want them to decorate with colors, they need to buy them at the office supply store and can keep them during the game. Three different colors, such as pink, green and orange highlighters, work well.

Timer – can be an egg timer or you can use a cell phone as most have timers on them now. Teams get 3 minutes to make the product, but it is best to be a little more lenient the first couple of rounds.

Paper – raw materials consist of both 8-1/2 X 11inch sheets of white paper and some sheets cut up in quarters (1/4 of an 8 ½ X 11 sheet) for making the products.

Paper Clips – these are used to weight the airplanes so they fly differently than without the paper clips.

Office Supply Store board – an 11X17 board that has a title and several items for purchase. You can use the PPT file with the items and print it as a handout with 9 slides to a page—then cut out and paste on the board. The title can be done with Word Art (in Word) and pasted on the top of the board. Lamination for an 11 X 17 board is around $4.00 at Kinko's/ Fed Ex Office store. To make the small items, set up slides in MS-PowerPoint™ and then print the PowerPoint™ file in color as a handout with 9 slides to a page and cut them out. Then use laminating sheets from an office supply store to laminate the items. Lastly, use sticky wall clay or clear sticky Velcro™ to put the laminated items onto the board's corresponding items.

Biz Ops Weekly Grid Facilitator Board – This is the same as the weekly grid that the teams use, but printed in an 11X17 format. Glue onto card stock or thin cardboard and laminate. Use a picture of an airplane or other symbol such as a stop sign; these can also be laminated using laminating sheets as they are used for the facilitator to move from day to day to guide the students.

After supplies are collected and in place, each team starts out with:

- One pattern for making an airplane (optional—you can also allow them to design their own airplanes—if you do create one or find one on the internet to use,

copy the template onto card stock and laminate with laminating sheets so you can reuse it.)
- One pen or pencil
- One Biz Ops Weekly grid (sample below)
- One role sheet (sample below)
- $200 in play money

Biz Ops Game™ – Activity Instructions
Before the game begins:

1) **Make sure the "what you need" above is completed.**
2) **The camp staff fills the following roles for the game (fill in the blank with staff name):**

_____Facilitator (times each of the activities and facilitates the game using the facilitation biz ops weekly grid). The facilitator needs to keep the simulation moving so that it doesn't drag on for too long.

_____Customer (buys the products from the salesperson); the customer needs to coach the sales person on sales techniques, handshakes, eye contact and give hints on what they want to see in the future such as more colors, or business cards (while the sales person is selling the product to them). The Customer role is the most crucial in making the simulation a success.

_____Banker (works with the team accountant by lending money and receiving loans and interest payments; they also keep track of who has paid back what so they know who may still owe at the end of the game).

_____The Wholesaler sells raw materials to the teams; the raw materials exist of plain white paper; they can buy a full 8 ½ X 11 inch sheet for $100 each or they can buy a cut one-quarter size of a 81/2 X 11 inch piece of copy paper; they are sold to the teams for $30 each.

_____Office Supply Store Owner sells office supplies to the teams from the office supply board; products and prices are listed on the office supply store board.

NOTE: if you do not have enough staff to fill all of the staff roles they can be doubled up. The customer and facilitator can easily be the same person, as can the Banker and the Wholesaler.

1) Set up the runway for the airplanes to fly on using duct tape (or other easily removable tape if the facility you are at does not want you to use duct tape). The runway should be approximately 15 feet long with an X that is approximately 12 inches long at the end of the runway.

Starting the Game (Main Facilitator/Instructor):

2) **Break down the group into teams of 4 -6 (depending on the size of the group)** – You can do this by table, numbering them off or by going around the room and having kids say, banana, orange, apple, peach, pear, grape, etc. Then direct the groups to their specific tables. Usually at the beginning of the week, I let them stay at their existing tables since they don't really know each other yet. The end of the week will depend; sometimes the kids want to be in the same

team they were in at the beginning of the week since they already know how to work together as a team. However, if I go into a classroom where the kids know each other well, I always have them count off. This avoids cliques being together and helps some of the others excel.

3) **Introduction to the Biz Ops Game™ (5 minutes)** – this should be done by the main facilitator of the activity, who should be assigned ahead of time so that they are familiar with how the simulation runs.

Points to include in the introduction:

a. It is a business game that simulates the weekly operations of running a business. **The goal of business operations is to keep the business running smoothly and to maximize profit.**

b. You are going to be running a transportation business that manufactures and sells paper airplanes. You will have a runway to fly your airplanes on; the straighter the better and if you land on the 'X' you will receive a $500 quality bonus. (Note: If you play the game later in the camp; you can use airplanes again or you can switch to helicopters or something that is created by the teams.)

c. There will be Customer Preferences—so you'll want to be sure to listen to your Customer!

d. You will start with a $200 loan from the bank and you will have to repay $240 at the end of the week (discuss that the $40 is interest and explain that all debt financing loans have interest that has to be paid in addition to paying back the loan).

e. Teams have the option to pay a portion of their loan back each day, and if they do so, they will reduce their interest repayment by $10 per day.

f. The team that makes the most money (net profit) and is ethical (good time to discuss what ethical is)—wins!

g. Each team receives a biz ops weekly grid to keep track of what they are doing for the week.

h. Each team receives a role sheet to assign roles to each member of the team and to know what the daily theme is.

4) **Create a Company Name** – Once the introduction to the game is complete; give the teams **2 minutes to think of a company name and have them to list it on their role sheet and on their biz ops weekly grid.** Then go around to each team and ask for their Business Names – write them on the white board or flip chart.

5) **Describe the Roles needed to run the business** – Have them write down descriptions on their role sheet. As you describe the roles, use questions as a facilitation tool by asking the kids what they know about each of the roles and what characteristics they think are necessary for each of the roles. Also explain that everyone on the team must have a role. Once

they are described, give the teams a few minutes to assign the roles for their team.

These roles should include:

Accountant – budgets for raw materials, savings and expenses, records information on the sheets (strengths: math and legible writing).

Financial Officer – goes to the bank for loans and makes deposits; this could also be the accountant if you don't have enough members on the team (strengths: communication skills, trustworthiness, and math).

Sales Person – sells product to the Customer (strengths: communication skills, persuasive skills, listening skills, negotiation skills).

Purchaser – purchases raw materials from the wholesaler; this could also be the shopper if you don't have enough members on the team (strengths: communication skills, math skills).

Shopper – goes to the office supply store to buy supplies for improving the products that the team is selling (strengths: math and loves to shop).

Designer – designs the products from an artistic point of view (strengths: art, visual, communication skills).

Engineer- helps with product design to create a quality product (strengths: visual, 3d, communication skills).

Entire Team – manufacture, decorate, and assemble products in allotted time frame.

6) **Overview of Business day** – Guide the teams using the Weekly Biz Ops Grid (as they follow along with

their own sheets). Do a quick 5-minute overview of the business day before teams actually start. Explain that each hour represents about 2.5 minutes.

Take a look at the following hour-by-hour plan for your business day:

Hour 1: Plan – mention that is always a good idea to begin each day with planning. In the game we will begin by planning how much to spend:

Materials – $30 per ¼ sheet or $100 per full 81/2 X 11 inch sheet.

Expenses – from the office supply store; think about what you might need—mention that they might want to send the shopper to check out the store. The customer will communicate to the sales person that they like lots of color, or that a specific color is their favorite color—the sales person will then need to communicate that to their team so they know what to buy for the next day.

Savings – are you going to tie up all of your money in making your product or are you going to put some away to pay back the loan quicker?

Hour 2: Buy raw materials; Purchaser buys materials from wholesaler based on what is budgeted.

Hour 3: Office Supply Expenses – the Shopper buys office supplies based on the budget. **Engineer** – the engineer may want to work on a design for the product by tweaking the pattern or creating a new one.

Hour 4: Make – in order for everyone to be on an even playing field, they are not allowed to start manufacturing their airplanes until Hour 4 is announced by the facilitator. They get 3 minutes. During first round they can be given a little more time so they can get used to working together (5 minutes total should be enough). Don't forget to use a timer or cell phone countdown. They need to work as a team to manufacture, decorate and test their airplanes. They can test them on the runway if they have enough time—some teams will figure out they can make one and then have another team member test it while they are making and decorating other ones (this is something they need to figure out on their own). On the role sheet, there is a theme for the day that they need to pay attention to since the customer will pay more for planes that portray the theme. If you decide to include a pattern for the plane, demonstrate how to make the airplane using the pattern. A pattern is not required for the airplanes, but it can help if kids don't seem familiar with how to make one. (You can find patterns for paper airplanes on the Internet.)

Hour 5: Lunch Break (Teams must be quiet for 30 seconds—start over if they make noise). The game can get loud and this gets the group quieted down again.

Hour 6: Sell – the salesperson sells products to the Customer. This is when the team flies the plane on the runway to demonstrate the quality aspect. The customer may give some specific requirements, so it is important everyone is listening.

Hour 7: Repay – the Financial Officer goes to bank if they are repaying part of the loan.

After your campers experience the hour-by-hour camp curriculum, the responsibility shifts back to you as the camp leader to conclude the curriculum with these important steps:

7) Review the curriculum by facilitating them through each day using the large board and the airplane graphic as the marker for where you are on the board. Have the other camp staff walk around and help teams to make sure they are getting everything recorded as they go along. Each day should not take longer than 10 minutes.

8) At end of the week each team needs to make sure their loan has been paid in full and then they need to total the number of items sold, their dollar sales, and count the money they have left which is their net profit or bottom line (good time to review these terms).

9) Ask each team to report their numbers and write them by their team name on the flip chart or white board.

10) Announce the Winning Team!

11) Debrief the game; ask teams what they learned along the way, what they might do differently, what challenges they had, what successes they had, etc.

With this in mind, see below for an illustration of the Biz Ops Weekly Grid that each team uses and the larger grid that is used to guide the activity. Go to: <u>http://eseedling.com/more-than-a-lemonade-stand-book/book-resources</u> *and use the password:* **MoreLemonade** *to download a form to use.*

Company Name
Our Company's success depends on our team!
Below is a sample of the role sheet used in the Biz Ops Game™:

Biz Ops Game™ Roles

Company Name: _____

Roles:

_____ Accountant – budgets, and records information

_____ Financial Officer – Goes to bank for loans & make Deposits

_____ Sales Person – Sells product to customer

_____ Purchasing – Goes to wholesaler for Raw Materials

_____ Shopper – Goes to Office Supply Store to buy supplies

_____ Designer – Designs artistically

_____ Engineer – Designs structurally

Entire Team – design, decorate, and assemble airplanes in allotted time frame.

<u>Daily Themes:</u>

Monday – International day

Tuesday – Social Media day

Wednesday – Eco Day

Thursday – Sports day

Friday – TGIF

For an example of the office supply store items *Go to: http://eseedling.com/more-than-a-lemonade-stand-book/book-resources and use the password MoreLemonade to download a color example.*

 Campfire Wisdom: Always make sure to have at least two camp counselors in the room with the kids. This alleviates problems with kids blaming a camp counselor for something that they didn't do. This is also important when a parent wants to discuss a problem that involves their child.

Defining Your Big Ideas

After gaining a fundamental understanding of the curriculum and program for your campers, and beginning the process of implementing it within your camp, you can then begin to define your big ideas and discuss them with your campers. In order for the kids to learn about entrepreneurship, it is important to facilitate a discussion of what an entrepreneur is and then start working on the campers' business ideas. It is important to discuss the characteristics and definitions of an entrepreneur so the kids understand the context in which to develop their own business idea. Some of the kids have a hard time deciding on what idea they want to pursue, so it is best to start on it the first day of camp. Also, the computer lab is only available a couple of times during the camp—the first one being on day 2, so the sooner they have their business idea decided, the sooner they can complete their business card and work on their business presentation. The campers should have their notebook and materials so that they can jot down notes and ideas during the videos and discussions.

To introduce what an entrepreneur is and does, there is a great video by Grasshopper, a virtual phone company, on their website at: http://grasshopper.com/idea/.[1] It is also on YouTube entitled Entrepreneurs can change the world—Grasshopper. Set up the video by asking the kids to write down 3 things that an entrepreneur does or is as they are watching the video.

The video has many points that lead to a great discussion on how to define an entrepreneur, including:

- Anyone can change the world
- One person can make a difference
- Talks about who built our world-parents, grandparents, aunts, uncles
- They may have come with very little or nothing except a single brilliant idea
- They were thinkers, doers and innovators
- Entrepreneurs change the way we think about what is possible
- They think about how life can be better and make the world a better place
- They see opportunities even in times of trouble

---

1   Video use Permission granted by Taylor Aldredge, Ambassador of Buzz at Grasshopper

- There is risk involved
- They change people's lives, create jobs, and fuel growth
- They're finding new ways to solve problems
- Entrepreneurs can be anyone, even you
- Create the job you always wanted and make a difference
- In the discussion make sure to emphasize that entrepreneurs create businesses using their talents and passions, and focus on the fact that entrepreneurs solve problems.
- After the 'what is an entrepreneur discussion,' it is time to move on to the camper's business idea. There is a short one-minute video on YouTube from Channel One news entitled "Teen Entrepreneur Wrap up" that is a great introduction on picking a business idea and getting started.
- *Key discussion points from the video are:*
- Find something unique that others aren't doing
- Find something you enjoy
- Make a plan—find out how much it will cost and how much you will charge to make a profit
- Keep your customers happy, but don't let them take advantage of you
- It's a lot of hard work
- You can make money and it is a good experience for future jobs and college applications

Now it is time to help the campers pick the right business idea. It is best to start with something that they love to do. If they are passionate about it, they will put more effort into it. Also, for starting up, they need to focus on ONE BIG IDEA! Picking more than one will just make it harder to create a clear message, market the product, perform the service, or create the product and sell it to make money.

Here are some questions for starting that will help the campers narrow it down; use these in a group discussion. The kids might even bring up additional ideas:

- ✓ Look around for problems that need solving
- ✓ What are your hobbies, interests & talents?
- ✓ What work-related experiences (mowing grass or shoveling snow) do you have?
- ✓ What have friends, family, teachers or coaches said you are good at?
- ✓ What do you think you are good at?
- ✓ What do you like to do in your spare time?
- ✓ What type of lessons have you taken (music, dance, or sport)?
- ✓ What type of sports have you participated in?
- ✓ What classes do you like in school?

Now that they have jotted down ideas during the discussion, they can start narrowing it down by using the '3-2-1 Exercise.' Some of the answers might be on more than one of the lists (it would be fantastic if the one big idea was all 3 lists). You can create a worksheet with the information below or just have them take notes and answer the questions below.

List 3 things you love to do:

List 2 things you are good at:

List 1 thing other people think you are good at:

List a problem that can be solved by something on the 3-2-1 list:

Once those questions are answered, encourage the kids to look at the list and see if there is anything they can do to earn money and solve a problem. Let them know people will pay for a product or service that solves their problem. In order to move forward with creating the brand and developing their idea further, they need to pick the "One big idea" that they are going to work on for the week. Let them know that is OK to have lots of big ideas, but that it is better to focus on one in order to develop it and learn from it before going on to the next.

They should also think about how much time they have available during the summer and school year to devote to their business idea. They can jot down on their worksheet the amount of time and what hours they are going to work on their business idea. This will increase the probability of it getting done—just as money has to be budgeted, so does their time.

Learning Business Basics

At the heart of the camp curriculum is the hope that your program will teach young entrepreneurs the fundamental business principles that will lay the groundwork for future endeavors. Business basics are broken into four sections and each section is assigned to one of the camp counselors to teach based on their interest and expertise. Each of the sections has information that the campers will use in their business plan that they present to their peers and on their posters that they create for the poster session. Each section has a total of 30 minutes of teaching involved. It is broken down during the camp into two different teaching segments of 15 minutes each. The content is taught in small groups of 4-5 students each. Each group is then rotated through the sections after 15 minutes each. The sections consist of basic financial, marketing, product or service creation, and customer service.

These modules prepare the students to put their business plan in action when they leave the camp. Some of the campers may choose to work on a business idea that they are not going to start now, but that is a "dream" business that they may start sometime in the future. This works fine but it is always good to see if you can encourage them to work on something that they can start on now. Explain that they will learn from it, so that when they get to their "dream" business they have learned some lessons that will help them succeed. The reason for breaking the sessions down is to provide variety in instructors, to get the kids to move around (from section to section), and to ensure they don't get bored from listening to one topic for a longer period of time. In each of the sections, you will want to set up worksheets with the information that is being presented so that the campers can have them in their binders or notebooks to refer to when they are applying it to their own business idea.

Campfire Wisdom: There are two 15-minute segments for each subject (in the same groups with the same camp counselor) during the camp so there is a total of 30 minutes on each subject. This allows each of the camp staff focus on their strengths so that they are more comfortable when teaching the content.

Section 1: Finances and Record Keeping (2-15 minute sessions)

The financial section starts with reviewing the basic definitions of

1) **Income**
2) **Expenses**
3) **Profit**

These terms were explained and discussed during the business simulation. They were also included in the pre-test and will be in the post-test. It is important that the campers understand how they relate to running a business. For purposes of keeping it simple, we define these terms as:

Income (or Revenue): Money you earn from selling your product or service.

Expenses: Money you spend to buy supplies for running your business or making a product.

Profit: The "Bottom Line" or your income minus your expenses.

Start-up Costs: the kids need to think about what they need to start up the business and how much it will cost. Then they can figure out where they are going to get the items or money if needed. This is important to include in their business plan; the kids will also work on start-up costs during the Team Lemonade Stand activity. This is also why it is important for the kids to have chosen a business idea to work on so that they can apply the concepts to their "big idea." Give them some examples of what startup items are so they can apply it to their own idea. (Examples include: Computer, Printer, Paper, Office Supplies, Business Cards, Marketing & Promotion, and Attorney fees, Permits or Licenses.) If they don't know the costs of the items they need, they can go to a store in the evening and check on prices, or they can search on the Internet.

Variable costs (COGS=Cost of Goods Sold): these are the next concept that is taught in the financial section. Just as it was important in the business simulation to know how much they spent on their raw materials to make their paper airplanes, it is important for the campers to know how much it costs to make their product or provide their service.

Start by defining the term and applying it back to the business simulation where the pieces of paper they bought to make the airplane were part of their Variable Costs or Costs of Goods Sold. The total variable cost is not only the paper; ask them what else they think it would include. Hopefully they will bring up their time, but if not you can ask them if they would like to work for free. They usually get it then! Variable costs are the total of how much it costs to make or buy each product or service you sell. Make sure you give them some examples.

Some common ideas you can include are:

1) For one bracelet: 1 hour of time, 10 inches of wire & 20 beads.

2) For one mowed lawn: 1 gallon of gas for lawn mower and 1 hour of time.

Of course, they will need to determine how much they will want to get paid (this will be covered in more detail later when the campers discuss how to determine the price of their service or product). Again, you will want to provide some type of a worksheet for the campers to write down their ideas, and list what they need for each product or service that they sell. The worksheet should also have a spot for the cost so that they can calculate their cost of goods sold and know what to price their product or service at in order to make a profit.

The campers will also need to know their *fixed costs* before pricing their product or service. Fixed costs are the costs needed to run a business. They are bills you have to pay on a regular basis, either monthly or annually. The kids may not have any of these, but it is still good to bring them up as they may have one or two (such as a phone bill); it also lets them know that if they grow, these expenses will have to be taken into account when pricing their product or service. Some examples to let the kids know about are: rent, electricity, phone, advertising, and loan payments. Let them know that Fixed Costs can also be called "overhead." The campers will need a worksheet to list any fixed costs they have.

Now that the campers know what their costs are, or have a good idea of what they might be, they need to determine if they will need more money to start their business. That leads into the next terms defined related to funding their business.

The terms included in the discussion on funding their business are:

1) **Bootstrapping** - Starting small, working hard and building slowly - you may need to get a job to earn some money first.

2) **Angel Investor** - Someone who invests in your business; could be a parent, grandparent or other family member (they usually want something in return such as payment or part of the company).

3) **Debt Financing** - borrowing money that is paid back with interest (this is the type of money that was used to fund the airplane company in the biz ops game™ they played). The discussion should include the advantages and disadvantages of each one so the kids know what their options are. Usually kids bootstrap by working another job such as babysitting or doing jobs around the house, but it is good for them to know what their options are if their business grows.

Since costs were calculated earlier in the session, the kids can now start to decide on the price of their product or service. To discuss selling price, it helps to show the kids an example of how the selling price affects their profit. Using a cup of lemonade as the product is an easy to understand example, and it will also be used later in the camp during the Lemonade Stand Competition. Asking the kids for their ideas on what happens when the price goes up (usual answers are more money, possibly less sales) and when the price goes down (usual answers are more sales, less money) is a great way to start before the example is shown.

The example below shows examples of different selling prices and profits:

Selling Price	Cups Sold	Total Income	COGS Per Cup	Total COGS	Total Profit
40¢	60	$24	20¢	$12	$12
50¢	50	$25	20¢	$10	$15
60¢	40	$24	20¢	$8	$16
70¢	30	$21	20¢	$6	$15
80¢	20	$16	20¢	$4	$12

Additional factors that need to be taken into account when pricing their product or service are the competition, the economy, and the price customers will pay. These factors should also be included in the pricing discussion. A good exercise is to have the kids ask the other campers what they would pay for the product or service. If that is not their ideal customer, then they should try to ask some adults that night so that can decide on a price. For the business presentation at the end of the week, the kids should include start-up costs (or at least the items), their cost of goods sold, any fixed costs, and profit per unit sold. There is a complete list included in the business presentation section that can be used as a guideline.

Section 2: Market Research and Promoting Your Business

The Marketing section is started by defining marketing as communication of the benefits of a product or service to potential customers. The customer has to have a need or want in order to be interested in buying a product or service. Some discussion about the 4 P's of marketing is a good way to start the section.

The 4 P's consist of:

1) Product - what you are selling (could be a product or service)

2) Price – the price of your product is based on costs, competition, and what people will pay

3) Place – where you are selling from (could be the Internet or an ideal location with potential customers)

4) Promotion – how you get the word out about your product or service

Ideally it's best to complete the ideal customer avatar and the competition section in the first 15-minute session, followed by the branding and promotion section in the 2nd 15-minute session. Once the marketing concept is introduced, the kids need to know who they are going to market to, meaning they need to choose an ideal customer. Avatar is a very popular word in games and it was a blockbuster movie, so starting with creating an ideal customer avatar is very relatable to the kids. Below is a sample questionnaire that can be used to come up with an ideal customer avatar.

Creating an Ideal Customer Avatar

To fully embrace and create an ideal customer avatar and both evaluate and understand your target markets preferences and customer makeup, begin by asking the following important questions:

How old are they?

Is my customer a business or a person?

If it is a business, what do they sell?

Are my customer's male or female, or both?

Where do they live? _____ in my neighborhood _____ in my city _____ in a rural area

How do they get from one place to another? _____ walk _____ car _____ bus _____ bike

How much money do they have to spend on products or services like the one I'm selling?

_____

_____

_____

What problems do they have?

_____

_____

_____

Do they have access to?_____ Internet_____ phone_____ cable/satellite_____ camera

What are their hobbies?

_____

What do they do for fun?

_____

What clubs do they belong to?

_____ _

What type of clothes do they wear?

_____

Additional facts about my ideal customer:

_____

_____

_____

List any potential customers you already know (friends, family, teachers, students, coaches, etc.).

Researching the Competition

After evaluating your potential customer base, the next thing that is covered in the marketing section is competition. It is important to know who the competition is so that the unique differences can be determined. Some questions that can be answered about the competition are: Who is my competition? What are their strengths and weaknesses? How much do they charge? How is my product or service different than my competition? and How is my business different than they are? Have them think about one or two things that they do really well and then have them rate their competition on a scale of 1 (worst) to 5 (best) on those things they are really good at. Then have them think about how they can do them even better. The kids can investigate their competition by visiting local businesses or by searching online and researching the questions above.

Once you find the one or two aspects you can do better than any of your competition, you will have your unique selling proposition. This is what is used to sell against the competition.

Benefits, Benefits, and More Benefits

Along with the unique selling proposition, it is important to come up with a list of benefits for the product or service. Benefits are important in persuading the customer to buy even if they have objections. The benefits can help sell against particular objections, so it is important to know several. A good way to come up with benefits is to brainstorm every problem the product or service solves. Then have them interview the other campers and the camp staff to see if they agree or have additional benefits that could be added to the list.

Branding

Branding is important, even for a small business because it is the impression you want to make on the customers—it is your reputation. The impression should communicate what is special about the business and should be positive. A brand should promote the business, connect with the ideal customer avatar, and differentiate you from others. Sometimes it is easier to think of your brand as a person, an identity. A good start to the brand discussion is to look at brands that kids can identify with and ask them how it makes them feel—what impression does the brand give them? Then have them work on their brand and create a product or service name and a possible logo that they could use when making their business card later in the camp.

Promotion

Once the brand is created, the kids will need to think about how to promote it. Promoting is about getting the word out on the product or service so that people know about it and will want to buy it. Some possible ways to promote are creating a website, building a social media page, creating a flier or brochure, and creating posters. Available money and time will have an impact on what can be done. The best way to promote a product or service is word of mouth; so asking customers to refer their friends and family is a great way to promote. Testimonials (reviews) from customers will also help promote the product or service, so ask customers if they will review the product or service. Another good idea is to collect names and contact information from customers and prospective customers. These can be entered in a spreadsheet, an email list program such as Mail Chimp (which is free up to a certain number of contacts), or in an email program such as MS-Outlook or Gmail.

Campfire Wisdom: There is a website entitled **www.bizkids.com** (from Biz Kids, LLP) that has great videos and resources for teaching business concepts. The videos are approximately 28 minutes long and have curriculum included. There is a section for students and teachers and sharing and use is encouraged on their website. They follow the national and state standards for entrepreneurship.

Section 3: Creating an Exceptional Customer Experience

After considering your fundamental business concepts and marketing plan, the next step is to diligently work towards to creating an exceptional customer experience. To create customer retention and ensure success throughout the life of your business, it is important to instill into your campers an attitude and focus towards a positive "customer experience." This section is included because without providing an exceptional customer experience, your customers may not return and worse yet may tell others their negative review. In the current day of social media that means they may tell thousands of friends in a matter of just a few minutes. The first thing that needs to be defined is, "What is an exceptional customer experience for my customers?"

In the first 15-minute session, the following videos should be viewed and discussed:

There are many videos on YouTube that show bad and good customer experiences. There is a FedEx video that went viral that provides a good example of bad customer service: http://youtu. be/PKUDTPbDhnA (this video has over 9 million views). FedEx did post a video response (Official Fed Ex YouTube channel) to the video that stated it did not match their company philosophy: http://youtu.be/4ESU_PcqI38 (even though it was a great video to try and make it right, there were only 574,000 views of the apology). This is great example of how everyone in the company is responsible for a great customer experience.

It is fun for the kids to watch the bad customer experience videos but it is just as, if not more, important to show the kids an example of an exceptional customer experience. The

Ritz Carlton Hotel has always been known for an exceptional customer experience, but this video (posted by Mercantile Capital Corporation: Joshie at the Ritz-Carlton) of the Ritz Carlton Hotel Amelia Island goes above and beyond: http://youtu.be/aH90uzU5YUw.

After both the bad and the good videos are viewed, discuss what the kids thought of the videos and what could have been done differently. Have them jot down some notes on what creates an exceptional customer experience. Tell them to start thinking about their own business idea and how they can provide an exceptional customer experience.

In the 2nd 15-minute session, they should have a worksheet that will help guide them in developing the exceptional customer experience that they want to create in their business.

The topics include:

1) **Responsibility**. Everyone is responsible—the company's reputation is based on every single person in organization (Fed Ex story).

2) **First Impressions.** First Impressions are crucial—you have a short time to make a first impression, so figure out the first thing you are going to do (how you will greet them, what your website will say about you, what your social media sites will contain).

3) **Customer Service**. Create a customer service Mantra for your company. A Mantra is a short saying you can say over and over (or post on the wall) that will focus your mind in a positive way. A good way to show this is to create some slides or a worksheet with examples

of customer service mantras of companies that the kids are aware of. For example Disney's is "Be our Guest"—they treat all customers like a guest. Have the kids work on one for their company; it should be included in their final business presentation and on their poster.

4) **Listen**. Actively listen to the customer—relate this concept back to the biz ops game™ played earlier in the week. Remind campers that the customer communicated to the sales person about different things that he or she liked, which helped the teams earn more money in the game. Discuss the importance of listening to the customer and stress that it will help them serve the customer better by giving them what they need.

5) **Communicate**. No matter what you do, you can't make everyone happy. It is important to come up with a plan for difficult customers. Clear communication will help with establishing deadlines and expectations. The more specific the better—early next week means Monday to one person and Tuesday evening to the next, so it is better to clarify. Difficult customers sometimes just want someone to listen to them, but it is good to have a plan of how to deal with them. What is their return policy or cancellation policy; will you give them something for free?

6) **Smile**. Customers do not want to work with grouchy people, so it is important to smile and have a positive attitude.

Once these important issues are discussed, have the kids write down the top 3 things they are going to do with their business to create an exceptional customer experience. These, along with the mantra developed earlier in this section, should be included in their business presentation and poster.

Section 4: Product and Service Creation

The last section that is taught in the camp curriculum is product and/or service creation. In the other sections the kids created an ideal customer, calculated the costs for making their product or service, researched the competition, and discussed how to market their idea. In this section the kids will discuss what they will actually create as their product of service so they know exactly what goes into it, so they can make sure it is something that their ideal customer wants, and so they can clearly communicate what it is to their prospective customers. In the first 15-minute session products should be covered, and then in the 2nd 15-minute session services should be covered. Also included in the second session is how to know if a customer wants their product or service.

Start by discussing the production process. Refer back to the Biz Ops Game™ played earlier; the discussion was centered on how the airplane was created. Ask campers what base materials were used (paper as the raw materials), what other materials were used to enhance the base design (paper clips, markers, scissors, ruler) and what labor was necessary to actually produce the airplane (folding or assembling, cutting, measuring, designing, decorating, and testing). These are all parts of the production process and need to be taken into account when producing a product. The kids who are creating a product should have a worksheet or a notebook where they write down what goes into the production process. They may want to refer back to their financial section notes where they should have written down the raw materials needed for their product.

Another topic of discussion is identifying the best way to purchase their raw materials. Again, this can be related back to the Biz Ops Game™ when the raw materials came in two different sizes, one large sheet or one already cut small sheet. There were advantages and disadvantages to both. The large sheet was less expensive over all, but scissors had to be purchased and used to cut it smaller, and it took more time to do this step. The smaller sheet was more expensive but it was already cut, so no scissors had to be purchased and additional time was not needed. These need to be taken into account when the kids are working on their production process.

Many of the kids will not be creating a product but will be providing a service. Some of the common ones I've seen are babysitting, lawn mowing, tutoring, music lessons, and sports lessons. The service needs to be packaged so that the customer knows what they are getting when they are purchasing the service. For example, if the service is tutoring and the price is $10.00 per hour, what is included in the service? Is it just time helping with the subject that the customer needs help with (and what specific subjects are focused on)? Do you include additional exercises the customer can work on to increase their knowledge when you are not with them? Another example would be lawn mowing, which would include things as pricing for different size lawns and whether trimming and other services are included in the lawn mowing service. These need to be clarified so that the customer and the business owner are in agreement of what the service entails. Again, a worksheet should be created, or the kids should write down what the service includes and what it's priced at.

Does the customer really want the product or service? This is something that should be covered with the kids so that they don't go out and spend a lot of time and money creating a product or service with no customer need. When creating a product, it is a good idea to let them know that many businesses create a prototype or a model of their product and then ask potential customers what they like and dislike about it, and possibly even what they would pay for the product. When creating a service, they may want to create a customer survey that describes their service and then ask potential customers what they like, what improvements they might make to it, how often they might use the service, and what they would pay. This will help guide the kids in the right direction so they are not wasting their time and not getting frustrated by creating something that won't sell.

 Campfire Wisdom: Copying each business section on different color paper is very helpful so that when working with the kids, you can refer to the blue section in their binder (or the green section, etc.). This makes much it easier and faster for the kids to find the materials and so you are not wasting time looking for the right pages.

Guest Speakers and Field Trips

To this point, we have discussed the internal workings of your camp. But externally, there are enormous opportunities to use local resources to enhance the learning experience. An important part of the camp is recruiting entrepreneurs as guest speakers and visiting local businesses on a field trip. When looking for speakers and businesses to visit, look for businesses that the kids would be interested in. Pick ones that have a product or service that the kids can relate to, or that have an interesting story. When planning the field trip you want to think about the locations of the businesses and the travel time it takes to get there; you don't want to spend your entire field trip walking or riding on a bus.

Once you target businesses, you will want to contact them and see if they would like to share their story and expertise with the campers, and whether they would want to come to the camp or if they would like you to visit the business. Let them know that 20-30 minutes is the ideal amount of time to speak or visit them. Then you will fit them into your camp schedule and communicate clearly when and where. It's always a good idea to remind the kids how to treat a speaker and how to respect the location where you are visiting. Also encourage the kids to come up with 3 questions that they might be curious about that they can ask the entrepreneurs. They may also want to bring their notebooks along to write down any ideas that they think of when they are on the field trips.

Before going on the field trip to area businesses, it is a good idea to discuss professionalism. The discussion includes how to be a good listener and how to respect the businesses and their owners, especially since they are volunteering their time and expertise. This is also a good time to talk about good business etiquette including appropriate dress, what makes a good handshake (along with time to practice the handshake), and being polite. It is very important not only to make a good impression, but also to build relationships that can lead to sales.

Short Games and Activities

Throughout your camp curriculum, you will find numerous occasions to implement short games and activities to build team morale, and offer insightful learning moments. These are quick and focused activities that usually introduce one very important and directed message. For example, from the first morning of camp, the campers can play the name game and the group resume game as introductory icebreakers to get to know each other better. It is a good idea to continue the introductions for at least the first two or three mornings of the camp.

Another icebreaker that is fun for the kids is the getting to know you thumball game at Trainer's Warehouse (www. trainerswarehouse.com). It's inexpensive and can be used over and over. Another option is to create a do-it-yourself getting to know you game by purchasing an inexpensive beach ball, blowing it up and using a permanent marker to section off the ball with getting to know you questions. Both of these games are played by tossing (not throwing) the ball to someone in the room and wherever their thumb lands, that is the question they answer. Once they answer the question, they toss the ball to someone else and then sit down. Once everyone has answered a question and is seated the game is complete.

There are a few other short activities that are strategically woven into the camp. They include professionalism, presentation skills, business ethics, and characteristics of an entrepreneur. Each of these short activities relates to a different portion of the camp and will be outlined in their respective passages below.

Presentation Skills

Since the kids are giving a 3-minute business presentation to their peers, it is important to include a short section on presentation skills. Using humor to present this subject works well. On YouTube there are many videos on bad presentations that can be used as examples of what not to do and what makes for a good presentation. There is a very amusing video posted on Don McMillan's YouTube channel entitled "Life After Death by PowerPoint 2012,"[2] https://www.youtube.com/watch?v=MjcO2ExtHso, on what not to do with PowerPoint. Another one that has been used is "Funny Presentation Training - How many errors can you find?": https://www.youtube.com/watch?v=wXILI9Q1jIw (posted on Booher Consultants— Effective Communication YouTube channel). The kids should jot down what errors they find and discuss the errors, followed by a discussion of what it takes to give a good presentation.

A good presentation mantra to keep in mind is: Breathe, Smile, Focus. Tell campers that everyone gets nervous, and talk about how you can use breathing to help. Discuss how a smile can help build a relationship, and how focusing can help keep you in the moment and not be distracted.

2   Video use permission for "Life After Death by Powerpoint 2012" granted by: Engineer/Comedian Don McMillan website: "www.TechnicallyFunny.com"

Then discuss what the kids should include in their own business presentations to tell a good story in 3-minutes. Talk about what they might want to include on the business poster that is presented to their friends and families. Below is a sample worksheet that can be used as a guide for the kids to use when they are planning their presentation and their poster. This is reviewed together as a group and then the kids will take a few minutes to finish the worksheet.

Circle the items below that you will include on your Business Poster and in your PowerPoint Presentation

Business Card   Mantra
Competitors   Who your customers are
Start Up Costs   Pictures of product/service
Prices   Customer pictures
Other (list below):

_____

_____

_____

_____

 Campfire Wisdom: After wasting many tri-fold poster boards from kids making mistakes on their posters, I came up with idea of taking a legal size piece of copy paper and making a model tri-fold sheet that they can use to plan out the poster before putting it onto the actual poster board. Implementing this step will save money because it costs much less to throw away a piece of paper than a poster board.

After the information is decided on, they can plan out their presentation. Below is a worksheet they can use to plan an outline for their presentation; this is also reviewed together as a large group. Then give the kids some time to work on completing the presentation plan so they can get feedback from the camp staff while they are working on it.

Title: _____

Who is the audience and what do they care about?

_____

_____

_____

What is the goal of my presentation?

_____

_____

_____

What are three main points I want to make?

_____

_____

_____

How will I begin my presentation?

_____

_____

_____

How will I close my presentation?

_____

_____

_____

What visual aids will I use to enhance my presentation?

❐ PowerPoint   ❐ Flipchart   ❐ Video

❐ Prezi   ❐ Pictures   ❐ Props/models

❐ Samples   ❐ Poster   ❐ Other:

 Campfire Wisdom: Before the kids give their presentations, remind them of the presentation mantra: "Breathe, Smile and Focus."

Business Ethics

The first year the Lemonade Stand Competition was introduced to the camp, there were a few students who put down the other teams and did not create a good impression for the camp, so business ethics were incorporated into the camp curriculum. Liberty Mutual Insurance has a great website entitled "The Responsibility Project" that has several great videos having to do with ethics. One that works great for the kids is called the Home Run: http://responsibility-project.libertymutual.com/films/the-home-run. It is a true story of how one team did the right thing and helped another team win a game because the other team truly deserved to win. The video creates a great base for a discussion on ethics and explains that being ethical means doing the right thing no matter what.

The discussion should then move to how doing the wrong thing can affect your business reputation and essentially put you out of business. Give examples and tell stories so that the students really understand. Emphasize that doing the right thing can give you and your business a positive identity and help your business to grow.

Characteristics of an Entrepreneur

One of the activities that the kids enjoy the most is going on the field trip to area businesses. A good way to debrief the field trip is to break the kids up into small teams of 4 or 5 and have them do a collaborative drawing with labels to create their own ultimate entrepreneur from what they learned during the field trip. A roll of long butcher paper works well for the drawing; they can cut it at a length that they can use to draw the entire entrepreneur head to toe. They might create labels that point to different parts of the entrepreneur such as intelligent (point to brain), creator (point to hands), visionary (point to eyes), flexible (point to knees), good communicator (point to mouth), good listener (point to ears) and on their toes (point to toes). The kids get 20 minutes to create their masterpiece and then each group explains it to the class. It is quite amazing what the kids come up with! After each group is done, facilitate a quick debrief on any important characteristics they missed.

The Lemonade Stand Team Competition

Much of the lessons learned during camp lead up to the culmination of the one or two week curriculum. The Lemonade Stand Competition is an exciting opportunity for your campers to demonstrate how much they learned by developing their concept and executing it in a "real world" setting. The Lemonade Stand has been voted as the #1 favorite activity by the campers since its inception. The activity is set up by telling the kids they are going to have the greatest lemonade stand ever. As they watch the two introduction videos, they are asked to write down 2 or 3 things that will make their team's lemonade stand a success. The 2 or 3 things will be used when they break out into their teams to work on their lemonade stand businesses. These should be kept confidential until they are in their own team, as they may become their competitive advantage.

The first video is called the "Lemonaire;" it was created by Umpqua Bank as a clever marketing campaign geared toward small and medium businesses. It is posted on Umpqua Bank's YouTube channel (http://youtu.be/RGk2qjlKsWs).[3] This video gives a fantastic overview of what goes into a start-up business (lemonade stand and otherwise). It starts out with the main character (Jonathan) getting laid off as a dog walker because the neighbors moved, and so he decides to start a business. He creates a business plan, tests the product, works on trying to find start-up funds, and ends up going to several banks before getting a loan. He builds his stand, has a major setback on opening day, and finally opens the stand and achieves his goal! The video will be informational and inspirational for the campers.

The second video is called "America's Best Lemonade Stand," and it is posted on the Associated Press YouTube channel at https://www.youtube.com/watch?v=7wCdU2NiyEI. It is about the Lemon Sharks lemonade stand in North Carolina; this stand was voted the #1 Lemonade Stand in the nation. They have several flavors, a punch card, a ring toss game, slushies, and they donate part of their proceeds to charity. Since the teams need to use their creativity when creating their own lemonade stands, this video gives them ideas about some things they might do differently. It also acts as an

---

3   Video use permission for "Lemonaire" granted by Kimberly Howland, Creative Strategies at Umpqua Bank.

excellent starting point for a discussion on donating part of their proceeds to charity, which can lead to a discussion about raising money for the camp scholarship fund with their own lemonade stands.

 Campfire Wisdom: The reason for putting videos into the curriculum is not only to enhance the content, but also to see how mesmerized the kids are whenever a video is played.

Once the videos are over, there is brief group discussion on what makes a good lemonade stand. Included is the concept of a trade secret (a special recipe, a special service) and how some of the things they jotted down earlier in the lesson may become one of their team's trade secrets. In order for the teams to utilize the individual strengths of their members, ensure that all of the necessary jobs and accomplished roles are also discussed. Roles were discussed earlier in the camp during the Biz Ops Game™, so this discussion is a detailed review since the Lemonade Stand Competition is a bit more complicated. Below is a list of the roles that are needed to run a successful lemonade stand. Once they break up into their teams, they will assign these roles to members of their team.

- Marketing—promoting the stand/theme
- Selling—selling with integrity
- Production—making and testing
- Accounting—keeping track of the numbers
- Customer Service—taking care of customers

- Logistics—set up and appearance
- Project Manager—ultimately responsible for the lemonade stand

After the roles are discussed, the ground rules are reviewed. Most likely, any location that the camp is held will have some specific rules that need to be followed. For instance, if there is onsite catering there may be a rule that only prepackaged lemonade can be used. There also may be rules about where the kids can sell the lemonade based on the insurance policy and people working in the building. There may be rules about where signs can be posted and how. These are important things that need to be researched ahead of time; the building administrator is usually the person to contact about the specific rules. The other rule that is emphasized is that all proceeds go to the Youth Entrepreneur Camp Scholarship Fund and that all team members must help clean up at the end.

After the administrative parts of the business are discussed, and the large group is still together, sales estimates are discussed. This is important because the teams have to come up with a shopping list by the end of the day and they have a budget of $50 (most teams spend under $20 for their supplies). Weather, time period for selling, what is going on in the building the day of the sale, serving size, and marketing efforts are also discussed so that the teams can make a decision on supplies and pricing once they are divided up. Just before the teams are divided up, review the expectations of what they need to complete by the end of the day:

1) a shopping list with specific instructions,
2) define roles & responsibilities,
3) come up with a name, logo, theme, and colors,
4) a marketing strategy and (if time)
5) pricing.

By now, the kids can hardly wait to get going in their teams. To divide them up into two teams, they should line up by birthdates (including the year). They need to do this on their own without any help from the camp staff (who are just observers). This is a very interesting activity since sometimes 1 or 2 leaders will emerge and it will only take a few minutes; other times there is no leader and it will take up to 20 minutes. After they are lined up, verify that they did indeed go in the correct order. Once verified, count them off by 1-2-1-2, so that there will two groups (1's and 2's) with at least 2 camp staff working with each group. This forces the kids to work with a new group and eliminates any unfairness of specific kids working together. It is a good idea to find a separate room for each team to work in so that they can keep their information confidential until the sale.

 Campfire Wisdom: If there is 15-20 minutes of empty time sometime during the camp before the lemonade stand activity, you can have the kids line up by birthdates and count off by 1's and 2's to create their teams. That way they can start working with their team on ideas.

In the teams, the kids will work on their company name, logo, colors, and theme. They also need to decide what is on the shopping list as far as flavors, what size and color of cups, straws, and any other decorations (such as a plastic table cloth or balloons) they might want to purchase. One of the camp staff is responsible for shopping for both teams and they should try to purchase things as inexpensively as possible. The money that is spent is the teams' startup costs. When the kids are thinking about selling their lemonade, encourage them to think about where they can sell besides their main location; encourage them to think about how they might do it. Decorated copier paper box lids with holes cut in them make great travel sales and delivery trays. Each team should be provided colored markers, 4 pieces of poster board, duct tape, and colored & white copier paper to start their decorations and marketing materials.

If signposts are available and taping signs on the wall is not allowed, then it is a good idea to provide an equal number to each team. The teams should also have a donation jar for the Youth Camp Scholarship Fund. For marketing, some ideas to share with campers are making flyers, business cards or coupons to give to potential customers. Some teams may even come up with the idea of taking advanced orders. Most teams dress in the same color to match their themes and they may even have costumes (one year we had someone in a gorilla costume).

On sale day, the kids have some final prep time and then 30 minutes to set up their lemonade stand, decorate the stand, make and taste test their lemonade, and get it ready to go. It's a good idea to provide the kids with 3 or 4 pitchers filled with water and ice, 3 big stirring spoons, and also a big tray of extra ice so that they can start making the lemonade right away. They will also need starting cash—usually $25.00 is a good amount, with a variety of change, including one dollar bills and five dollar bills. The kids should have tally sheets for the quantity they sell at the main location, and with the traveling sales teams, to keep track of what they are selling.

Once the sale begins, the kids start selling, making, etc. for a full hour. It is a good idea to have a ballot box and ballots where the customers can vote for the best lemonade, best display, and best customer experience. That way if the kids don't sell the most or make the most money, they still have a chance to win one of the other categories. Once the hour is done, the kids clean up, the money is counted (both sales and donations), and the cups sold are totaled. Then the startup costs and the beginning cash are deducted from the total money. The results are given to the camp staff member who helped with the team. Once the teams are back in the main room, the activity is debriefed by discussing what worked and didn't work, and what they learned from the activity. Then the results are revealed. Ending with the total of what was raised for the Youth Entrepreneur Camp Scholarship Fund works great because then the kids don't think as much about who sold more or who made more money.

Campfire Wisdom: The kids never win the lemonade stand competition by the quantity of lemonade sold; it is always based on the donations raised. When coaching the teams it is important to emphasize that the goal of the activity is to raise funds for the scholarship fund and that it should be promoted on all the marketing materials.

The Lemonade Stand Team Competition offers campers a "real world" like experience. The fruits of their hard work and the results of all they learned come to life in an exciting and friendly competition that promotes teamwork, builds friendships, and instills the opportunity surrounding entrepreneurship. Most of your campers will leave this exercise feeling rewarded and enthusiastic about what they accomplished. Support the competitive spirit and ensure you take the time to offer valuable and positive feedback to each one of your campers to further nurture the seeds of entrepreneurial spirit that have been planted.

Business Presentations

On the last day of camp, each of the kids gives their business presentation that they worked on during camp. They should already have an outline that they prepared during the presentation skills section, and should have most of the content created during the business sessions and in the computer lab. The kids are also given a presentation checklist to use as they are developing their presentation so they know what will be good information to include in their presentations. This will help them with both their presentations and their posters.

Below is a sample checklist to use:

My Business Presentation Key Points

Guideline for information to use on my poster and presentation to the class

Introduction

- ❏ Business Name
- ❏ My name and title
- ❏ What is the product or service?
- ❏ What makes my product or service unique?

Marketing

- ❏ Who is the target audience?
- ❏ Why will they be interested in your product/service?
- ❏ What is your value proposition, i.e. what will make them buy from you?
- ❏ How will you promote to your target audience?

Customer Experience

- ❏ What are your customer experience mantra, mission & vision?
- ❏ What will you do to provide a good customer experience?
- ❏ What can you offer that your competition can't?
- ❏ How will you deal with demanding customers?

Product or Service Creation

- ❐ What is needed to create the product or service?
- ❐ What type of equipment & labor do you need?
- ❐ How will the product or service be delivered?
- ❐ Quality Control

Finance

- ❐ What are my start-up Items and costs?
- ❐ Costs per Unit of Service or Product
- ❐ Competitor pricing
- ❐ Sales price per Unit of Service or Product
- ❐ What is my Projected Profit?

You can go to: http://eseedling.com/more-than-a-lemonade-stand-book/book-resources and use the password: **MoreLemonade** to download the form for your program.

It is always a good idea to review what makes a good audience before the kids start their presentations. To keep the kids from getting bored, each of the presentations should be no longer than 3 minutes in length and there should be a break half way through. There will be some kids who will not want to present, so you may have to help them get through it, but it is important they go through with the presentation so that they feel a sense of accomplishment.

In preparation, and to ensure the presentations go quickly, number a flip chart or a whiteboard with the number of kids and have them sign up first thing on presentation day. That way, they know when they have to go and can be "on deck" and ready. The other thing is to have all of their presentations in the same directory or on a thumb drive so they can be pulled up quickly. If they are using Prezi, the Internet should be ready so they can just login and pull up their presentation. Generally the kids enjoy this part of the camp, and it is always fun to hear all of their ideas.

Before the Camp Ends

There are three things that are completed the last morning of camp before the business presentations. The three are outlined below:

1) **Camp evaluations** – it is important to get the kids to fill out the evaluations before they leave camp. I've tried to email them after camp and the completion rate is very low. The kids may give you a great comment that can be used for next year's marketing copy. You should already have a 'permission to use form' that was collected at the beginning of the camp, so it is not a problem to use their comments as testimonials.

2) **Thanks-You's** – it is important to explain to the kids how many people it takes to make the camp a success, and it's good practice in business and in life to thank people when they help you out. The easiest way I've found to do this is to make a list of all the people that need to be thanked and then make pieces of paper with their names on them. Put their names into a container and have the kids pick 2 or 3 names (depending on how many people there are to thank)

and write at least a paragraph thanking them for their help with the camp and maybe include one thing they learned at camp.

3) **Post-Tests** – if you are testing the kid's knowledge of what they learned at camp, they should complete a post-test, which is the same test they took at the beginning of the camp. This shows how much they progressed through the week.

Poster Session and Awards Ceremony

Parents always enjoy knowing what their kids worked on during the camp, so having a poster presentation and awards ceremony is a great way to communicate what the kids accomplished and to award the kids for their hard work. During the week, each camper creates a poster that displays information about their business. Each kid stands by their poster during the presentation and answers questions about their business. What works well is having the kids gather all of their materials and information, put it in their brief case, and then move the tables to the perimeter of the room. Then the chairs are moved in rows facing the projector screen, so their family members can sit and see the posters. The posters are placed on the tables around the room and kids can put their materials under the table where their poster is displayed.

The families and kids really like seeing the pictures taken during the week, so it is a good idea to create a slide show that you can play during the ceremony. At the ceremony, the camp director can give a short overview of the week's activities and then each kid is awarded a certificate of completion and their completed business cards. Of course, they will finish the way they started, with a business handshake. It's nice to have a cake and refreshments if your budget allows.

Section IV

Breathe: After the Camp is Over

||||||||||||||||||||||||||||||||||||||||||

S o you survived your first More Than a Lemonade Stand™ camp? Congratulations. But your work isn't complete. Often times, we camp leaders rest on our laurels and forget that as leaders, we have a duty to constantly try to improve. The hope is that your next camp will be better than your last. To do that, it is crucial you take the time post camp session to take a deep breath and then reflect on your camper's experience. That calls for assessment, analyzing, evaluation, and obtaining direct feedback from the campers, their parents, and your staff. With that said, considering the following steps after camp will help you to be attentive to the details and improve the quality of your future camper's experience:

Parent Evaluations. Parent feedback is also an important part of evaluating the camp; after all they are the ones who are paying for the camp. After the camp is over, send out a parent evaluation with a stamped return envelope. Parents often give great testimonials that can be used in the marketing copy for next year's camp (be sure to ask for permission to use on the evaluation form).

Debrief. After the camp is over, it is a good idea to have a follow-up meeting with the camp staff within two weeks of when the camp ends. It is nice to have some reflection time, but not too much time that things are forgotten. This is the time to discuss what worked and what didn't and to suggest any changes to make for the next year. If changes are to be made to some of the content or procedures, it may be easier to make the changes now while the camp is still fresh in your mind.

Storing Supplies. It saves a lot of time for the next year if you organize and inventory the camp supplies after the camp is over. It also helps to know what you will need for next year so you can watch for sales and save money. The supplies can be stored in labeled boxes or plastic containers.

As the title More Than a Lemonade Stand™ indicates, the camp utilizes the basic lemonade stand scenario as a building block for young entrepreneurs to start their business. But it is much more than a camp; it is a tool to help you teach entrepreneurship to the youth of today; to spark that entrepreneurial spirit so it will live on and change our world tomorrow.

More Than a Lemonade Stand™ is a reference tool that you can use year and after year to help kids realize that they are important and that they have the ability to utilize their own unique gifts, talents, and skills to create a business and help control their destiny. The activities are organized so you can choose them based on your own unique needs, or use the program as a whole. There are many great resources and activities available on the Internet, in bookstores and in libraries; I've included some of my favorites so you don't have to spend time searching, reading, and basically reinventing the wheel. When choosing a resource or using an activity, I advise that you test them out and then choose the ones that speak to you, that work for your situation, and that you feel passionate about so that you can be authentic and use that authenticity to help teach the kids that they can use entrepreneurship to make a difference.

About the Author

||||||||||||||||||||||||||||||||||||||||||||||||

I have always been a teacher at heart! Have you heard the saying, look back at what you played when you were a little kid (we actually tell this to kids at camp) and it will lead to your true passion and purpose? Well, when I was a kid, I played school and I was always the teacher. Now, my brothers may tell you that it was because I was the bossy big sister, but I will tell you it's because I loved to teach. Now that I look back, I realize that I have always loved teaching. I have a true belief that anyone can do anything they put their mind to (thanks Mom). If someone doesn't get it, I take it on as a challenge and break it down and help them learn. This has guided me my whole life; I've been a camp counselor, a religious education teacher, an aerobics teacher, a dance teacher, a scout leader, a choreographer, and a corporate trainer. When I went to college, teaching still continued to guide me as I obtained a B.S. in Elementary Education (grades 1-8) from the University of Wisconsin-Madison. Unfortunately, the job market didn't agree with my choice and I just didn't see subbing in a classroom as a viable financial choice, so I decided to go back to school.

I obtained a degree in Accounting and Data Processing (that's what they called computer science way back when) from a local business college (Madison Business College). This led me in a completely different path of computerized accounting systems where for the next 15 years, I helped companies take their manual business systems and convert them into the computerized world. Even though I was working with accounting systems, I was training business staff on how to use the systems, both in the classroom and one-on-one.

When I was 27 years old, I was fortunate enough to have a client (who became an angel investor) talk myself and a co-worker into starting a new company called Checks + Balances, which was a low cost alternative for small to medium-sized businesses to obtain accounting system implementation and support (much less than the CPA firm cost). In the three years that I started and ran Checks + Balances, I learned more than in any other period in my life. I learned how hard entrepreneurship was and how rewarding it was all at the same time! Then Check + Balances was sold to a larger consulting firm where I went to work for the next five years. I worked with larger companies, training their staff, upgrading their systems, writing custom reports, working many hours and traveling regionally 2 days a week. When I was expecting my 2nd child, I decided that it was too much, so I took another opportunity and became the

Director of Operations at a Management Consulting Firm based in Madison.

I had a flexible schedule and was fortunate enough to volunteer in my son's classroom one day a week; it was then I realized how much I missed working with kids. So when the company was sold, I looked into going back to school to update my teaching certification. During this time, I started working at the University of Wisconsin-Madison Small Business Development Center (SBDC) as the coordinator of the statewide Wisconsin Business Answerline, which answered questions for people starting or growing a business in Wisconsin. I completed a M.S. in Curriculum & Instruction (educational communications and technology) from the University of Wisconsin –Madison only to find out that schools don't want to hire someone with a Master's because teaching is unionized and they have to pay more for teachers with advanced degrees. So I continued to work at the SBDC and moved into managing educational programs and overseeing the entire event-planning department. I also created courses, became a Franklin Covey facilitator, completed my online teaching certification through University of Wisconsin –Extension, and taught business courses. Additionally, I helped with the Youth Entrepreneur Camp that we had for middle-school aged kids. We hired a consultant to come teach so my role was just assisting with the camp, but I loved sharing my entrepreneurial and teaching expertise and most of all working with the kids.

Then finally came the chance of a lifetime! The SBDC funding was cut and therefore the director said that we would have to cancel the camp (since it was not part of the SBDC's core mission). I was devastated; but entrepreneurship is about taking problems and making opportunities so I proposed to rewrite the curriculum so that we could teach it using our existing staff. He said yes, and that is exactly what I did in 2008. During the first few years I made changes based on feedback and what was learned, but for the past 4 years, the same planning process and curriculum has been used (which is the basis for this book). The camp has been such a huge success—we have kids from all over the country come to the camp and there is always a wait list. I get calls from all around the United States asking about how to put together a youth entrepreneur camp, so what better way to start than to write a book teaching others how to do it? Looking back through all of my experiences with teaching, working with businesses, and being an entrepreneur, I have adopted the philosophy that actions speak louder than words. It is my firsthand experiences working with children and in the business world that qualify me to write this book.

CPSIA information can be obtained at www.ICGtesting.com
Printed in the USA
BVOW05s0730131215

430130BV00004B/50/P

9 781630 474546